Stories, Food, Life

from North Country Public Radio

Editor
Ellen Rocco

Food Editor
George Arnold

Photography
Nancie Battaglia

Design
Steve Keetle

Chef George Arnold at work in his SUNY Potsdam kitchen. Nancie Battaglia

NCPR News Director Martha Foley and Morning Host Todd Moe sample one of Chef George's omelette entrees live on the air. Dale Hobson

North Country Public Radio informs, enriches and connects the communities of our region...on air, online, in your community.

Copyright © 2008 by North Country Public Radio
Photos Copyright © 2008 by Nancie Battaglia
Published by Adirondack Life, Inc., Jay, New York
ISBN-13: 978-0-922595-37-2

north country public radio
STORIES · MUSIC · LIFE

St. Lawrence University
Canton NY 13617
877-388-6277
www.ncpr.org

On the cover: *Small Farm, Tupper Lake.* Nancie Battaglia

Table of Contents *(recipes are italicized; essays and tips are not)*

Autumn, 64

Acknowledgments

Here's how this book came together.

In mid-2007 we were planning events and activities for the station's 40th anniversary celebration, in 2008. We thought a cookbook could bring people together from across the station's large service area.

We formed a committee.

Early in the process we decided two things: we wanted personal stories about food as much as we wanted recipes, and we needed a food editor.

We began soliciting recipes, stories and photos on our airwaves and Web site. We figured out we needed a book designer and a photographer. A little later, we realized we didn't know much about book publishing, which meant we needed a publishing partner.

Bit by bit, a year's worth of ideas, anecdotes, recipes and images began to emerge. And then we realized we did have a book, a real book from the Adirondack North Country, a mix of stories and recipes from peoples' lives and the history of this place.

Here are the people who gave so much time and talent to the project. We thank all of you.

THE FOOD EDITOR: George Arnold, chef and food historian, who works magic with even the most humble ingredients and who has transformed the SUNY–Potsdam food service.

THE PHOTOGRAPHER: Nancie Battaglia, world-class woman with a camera, who jumped in with her extraordinary library of work and knowledge of the region.

THE PUBLISHER: *Adirondack Life* magazine, whose staff, led by creative director Elizabeth Folwell and copy editors Lisa Bramen, Niki Kourofsky and Annie Stoltie, kept assuring us that there really was a wonderful book hiding in the piles of paper and navigated us through the arcane world of the print medium.

THE DESIGNER: Steve Keetle, who remained calmly encouraging at all times and who brought his creativity—sensitive and dynamic—to the task of figuring out what a radio station looks like.

THE COMMITTEE: Phil Harnden, who took on the first sorting of the tangled submissions and brought the resources of GardenShare to the book; Lynn Ekfelt, who contributed her insight as the editor of an award-winning regional cookbook to the process; and Carol Berard, who contributed her remarkably good instincts about food and books to the table.

THE NCPR STAFF PARTICIPANTS: News Director Martha Foley, editorial and artistic guidance; Web Master Dale Hobson, advice, Web-delving and humor; Web Assistant Rachel Henderson, research and copy editing; Production Manager Joel Hurd, for the companion CD, complete with his original music and guitar chops; Membership Director June Peoples (it really was your idea).

THE COMMUNITY: This book would be a pamphlet without the contribution of recipes, stories and photos from the many listeners and Web users who shared pieces of their personal and neighborhood food lives with us.

We are honored and grateful to have the apt and generous words of Bill McKibben and Michael Pollan inside the covers of our book.

Here's who believed in the project enough to help pay for it.

THE RIVENDELL FOUNDATION

ASGAARD GOAT CHEESE FARM, AU SABLE FORKS, NY

THE FOOD BANK OF CENTRAL NEW YORK, UTICA, NY

Special thanks to St. Lawrence University for always being there for the station.

Thank you, friends. Now that we're all here, let's eat.

Ellen Rocco, NCPR Station Manager, Canton, NY, 2008

I believe I am well qualified to write a few words here because I have stuck large quantities of local food in my belly, and large quantities of local radio in my ear, and found that they go extraordinarily well together.

In fact, it's no accident that both are booming. Around America, the fastest growing part of the food economy is local farmers' markets—their numbers double every few years, and sales rise faster than Walmart or Costco. And while Clear Channel struggles to hang on to the listeners for Corporate Rock and Know-Nothing Talk, public radio, community radio and low-power FM are growing like zucchini.

Why is that? Well, in both cases the ingredients are fresher and more nutritious. No high-fructose corn syrup in these recipes, just the kind of seasonal fare that brings out the most creativity in a chef. And on North Country Public Radio? No preprogrammed music, just the blues and roots music and bluegrass and regional talent and vintage wax and world music seasoned with hometown voices.

But it's not just the ingredients. It's also the community

that builds when we rely on our neighbors, not on some distant and anonymous source. Forget the Sysco truck rolling up to the restaurant—here are recipes from real people and local chefs, who often know the farmers who grew the ingredients. And the shopper at the farmers' market? On average, he or she has 10 times as many conversations per visit as the average supermarket shopper. Ten times! And if they're in Canton or North Creek or Old Forge or Westport or Saranac Lake, chances are the conversations concern the story from that morning's report by Brian Mann or David Sommerstein, or the conversation between Curt Stager and Martha Foley, or the book chat with Ellen Rocco, or the latest bad pun from Radio Bob.

In the world that's coming—the world where $5 gas makes us think differently about shipping the average bite of food 2,000 miles to reach our lips—we're going to need our neighborhood farmers again. It won't be a sacrifice—we'll be healthier for it in every way. Just like we've been healthier for the last 40 years because of North Country Public Radio. It's a local world again all of a sudden, and we live in one of its finest corners.

Right: *Farmers' market, Keene Valley.* Nancie Battaglia

One spring a few years ago I came across artichoke seedlings at a specialty nursery. Not Jerusalem artichoke, *artichoke* artichoke. I love artichokes. So I bought a few and actually harvested half a dozen small artichokes at the end of the summer before frost killed the plants. In Mediterranean and similar climates, artichokes are a perennial. They thrive. Growing artichokes in the North Country was like an earlier experiment with growing peanuts. Fun, but not something to count on or invest in too much. Unlike the virtual world, where you can happily marry images of camels with ice skaters under a Norwegian sky, geography matters in the three-dimensional world. The North Country is a real place, with mountain hamlets, river valley farms and frost possible in every month of the year.

Ellen Rocco with neighbor Aldena Conklin in the Conklins' chicken yard, 1973, DeKalb. Photographer unknown

When I arrived in the North Country—late February, snow up to my chin, old farmhouse, a tiny woodstove, no insulation—straight from Broadway in New York City, you could say I was, like the Pilgrims, dependent on my native neighbors for survival. Enter my nearest neighbors, Aldena and Milan Conklin, a quarter of a mile up the Maple Ridge Road, and still living very close to the land, very pre-World War II. They had raised six children in a two-story 12-by-12 house they built themselves,

Cow tails, Franklin County Fair, Malone. Nancie Battaglia

supporting all with a herd of 15 to 20 hand-milked cows. I learned how to milk from them, and a lot more. Aldena taught me about gathering wild food, when to plant a garden and, perhaps most important, how to can and store what I gathered and grew. For many years it was not unusual for me to put up hundreds of jars of vegetables, fruit and meat, plus fill a large chest freezer, and dry herbs, seeds, apples. Later, with my family gone, I cut way back on the canning and freezing. Now I'm back at it in full force, having come to believe that all those back-to-the-land instincts about providing one's own food, as much as possible without the help of agribusiness, made great good sense: not only cost-effective and healthy but, in words we didn't exactly use back then, an essential part of living green.

My early gardens were productive, but there was a learning curve—I now grow just a foot or two of green onions and a whole row of peas, rather than the reverse (yes, I grew 25 feet of green onions in my first garden). But having a garden was a miracle. You put a seed in the ground and … it grows into a zucchini! I am still astounded every year at how much food emerges from a modest farm garden. Actually, I'm awestruck. Remember, I grew up on the 18th floor of an apartment building. Seeds, soil, rain, sun … food. Amazing.

In the '70s, my work schedule allowed me to spend many summer hours with Aldena scrambling around the pastures, meadows and woods with the aim of bringing something back for the kitchen. In spring it was cowslips, wild leeks, morel mushrooms and even dan-

Produce stand near Malone. Nancie Battaglia

delions for wine. Summer began with the two of us, plastic containers and pots in hand, crawling around on south-facing hillsides picking wild strawberries for fresh eating, pies and jam. We picked enough of that tiny fruit for jam! Imagine. And we had time to clean the berries, sitting and chatting on the porch or under the shade of a maple. Later in the season we'd pull on long pants and long-sleeved shirts, tie buckets around our waists and head out for the blackberry patches. I associate late summer with burlap sacks, which we'd bring on our treks around the fields to fill with apples we gathered from all kinds of trees—Duchess, Pound, Yellow Transparent and many unnamed but loaded with fruit we shook to ground. There were two presses on the road, set up each fall for anyone who wanted to make cider or start vinegar. Other piles of apples would be cooked down for applesauce or sliced and dried; we ate fresh apple pie and crisps and muffins almost every day.

In September, Aldena and I would grab the buckets again and gather wild grapes from roadside vines for jelly. In years when grapes are bountiful, I still make wild grape jelly. People driving by stop and ask what I'm doing. They're always surprised. "You can really pick enough of those sour little grapes for jelly?" If I know where they live, I'll bring them a jar by way of proving it's worth the picking, cleaning and cooking.

There was a time when gathering, as well as growing, was a given—indeed a gift—for rural folk. Now, people may think I'm odd, but, oh my! You don't know how good it is until you grab a pail or sack and just head out on a beautiful day, returning with something wonderful to eat. I still think it's one of the miracles of living in the country.

Logging white oak, Burns Road, Redwood, 1979. From left, Frank Peters, John Scarlett and David Duff. Mark Scarlett, Rossie

It was early in my first January here when I decided to bring some vegetable bean soup to Aldena and Milan. I had a 1930s Home Comfort wood cookstove that I'd bought for $10, thanks to Donny Stevens, whose mother wanted it out of her woodshed. Like old pianos, cookstoves were often available just for the moving. (That wonderful stove lived with me for decades, but was just recently sent to a metal recycler and replaced by a Pioneer Princess, sold to us by an Amish neighbor for considerably more than $10.) I was still on the low end of the learning curve when it came to cookstoves. The previous November, my first Thanksgiving in the North Country, I had attempted a turkey in the Home Comfort. Let's just say lots of people enjoy that holiday meal in the early afternoon and we sat down to dinner around 11 pm—unintentional tectonic-creep-style slow cooking. By winter I was doing better at tending the fire and controlling the oven. The pot of bean soup we ate Tuesday evening was pretty good—lots of frozen, canned and dried ingredients from our pantry—but there was way too much of it. Unfortunately, I had seen too many old Westerns and episodes of the Waltons where the kitchen scenes always included a pot of soup steaming away on the back of the big stove—for days. I didn't check under the lid when I walked the pot up to Aldena and Milan on Thursday morning. Milan looked in it and asked if the green fuzz was supposed to be there. Refrigeration, even in the middle of a frigid North Country winter, is not optional. These days, for the steamy stove effect, I keep a teakettle going.

My mistakes as a beginner in the country remind me that there are skills needed to grow food, skills that have been largely lost outside of rural communities.

This is a food book. A food book put together by people who live in
the North Country. I've taken you through the seasons of my early years here because we all know that seasons make a difference in the country, in places where people are still connected to nature every day of the year, not just during two-week vacations. This book follows the seasons with stories and recipes that belong in the North Country. We didn't make up any rules for contributors to follow, but we selected material that comes from living in the North Country and will make sense to you if you have a kitchen or a garden or just spend time in this corner of the world.

There's a new generation of people who care deeply about food that comes from local sources, people who are involved with community-supported agriculture and diversified farming, people who want to eat food that tastes like food—all of which restores my optimism about those back-to-the-land impulses to grow it ourselves, right here.

Summer

There's something about summer that brings out the child and hearkens back to ancient inclinations. We want to cook out-of-doors over an open fire and eat with nothing but fingers and teeth. We want to gather in crowds, tumble in the grass and feast beneath the trees. We want mounds of chicken hot from the grill, sweet corn delivered at a run from the field to the pot. To cool the sweat, we want gallons of sweet iced tea with lemon, sharp frosty beer and an endless supply of ice cream, churned up on the spot.

The farmers' markets explode with bounty—homemade pies, artisanal breads and farm-fresh cheeses competing with just-picked pro-

duce. One could live the whole season, and except for coffee and the checkout tabloids, never need to enter a supermarket. There are berries free for

Gathering, Connery Pond. Nancie Battaglia

the picking in jealously guarded locations. There are hot dogs at the ballpark, shore dinners and parties at the camp, ice-cream socials at schools and churches, firemen's field days, backyard barbecues by the thousand, bullhead feeds, potluck dinners and pancake breakfasts.

If North Country summers were twice as long, no one would move to California. They'd hardly be able to move at all. —**Dale Hobson**

Left: *Cone for two, Donnelly's Ice Cream, Saranac Lake.* Nancie Battaglia

Summer Icons:

corn, tomatoes, berries ... okay, zucchini ... and fresh vegetables of all kinds. Eat your meat and dried beans come winter. Plenty of time for that. I think of my old neighbor Milan who had a saying for every situation, kind of a walking farmers' almanac. If the cows are lying down, it's a sign of rain; if the moon holds water (i.e., crescent-shaped and tipped up), it's a sign of drought. I have done no scientific testing of these adages, but I do firmly hold with the classic make hay while the sun shines—and be sure to eat sweet corn while you can. **—Ellen Rocco**

Above: *Tom Tucker on his Farmall, Gabriels.* Nancie Battaglia

Campfire Sweet Corn, *Yvona Fast, Lake Clear*

One of my favorite ways to prepare corn is over a campfire. Remove excess silk from the tip and soak the husks in water for at least a half-hour. Roast over the coals so the kernels steam a little. The husks will char in the fire, but the corn inside will be moist and tender. Remove the corn with tongs, peel back the husk, remove the silk, eat the pure sweetness and throw the cob and husk back into the blazing fire.

Golden Bantam Sweet Corn, *Mason Smith, Long Lake*

What I miss most about the good old days in the North Country is Golden Bantam corn. Back when we plied our way between Gouverneur and Hopkinton, many of the farms along the road grew sweet corn and sold it by the 13 ears. Golden Bantam tasted like the very essence of corn. For me, it's been sad to lose it in favor of these too-sweet, less-corny corns.

Sweet Corn on the Cob, *Cheryl Craft, Lake Placid*

Sweet corn tastes great if you husk it, grill it briefly on all sides until golden, then squeeze on lime juice and sprinkle on salt. If you have older corn that's past peak, this is a great way to redeem it.

Sweet Corn with Olive Oil, *Tom Akstens, Bakers Mills*

Corn with extra virgin olive oil and freshly ground black pepper.

Corn Pancakes, *Robin Rhodes-Crowell, Pierrepont*

A tradition of my family while growing up was to make corn pancakes. This was done simply by taking pancake batter (for my mom it was Bisquick; for me it is homemade whole wheat) and adding fresh raw corn (cooked or frozen won't do). I take the corn off the cob with a knife and add it to the already made batter. I splurge every summer by making a big batch and eating it all by myself—covered in maple syrup, a perfect match.

Keeping Corn Warm, *Sarah Cohen, Old Forge*

To keep corn on the cob warm, put a tea towel on a platter and wrap the cobs in the towel. The corn will stay hot throughout the whole meal, making it easy to apply lots of butter.

Corn Boats, *Jenny Walker, Potsdam*

When I was 15, I was offered a summer job taking care of a family and their guests at a Great Camp on Upper St. Regis Lake in the Adirondacks. My job was quickly transformed into cooking, and I kept this position throughout my high-school years. I spent those summer days playing in the kitchen and feeling very creative and passionate about food, searching for new preparation methods for various ingredients. Everyone loves corn, but how could I make it taste delicious as well as visually appealing? That was the day corn boats were born.

I remember serving the corn boats that first night. The dinner table, with seating for 20, stretched from one end of the room to the other with a massive hearth at the head of the table. Dinner was served buffet-style on an antique sideboard in the corner of the dining room. After setting out all the platters, I rang the dinner bell. A short time later, I heard sounds coming from the dining room: "Mmmm!" Corn boats became a weekly staple at the dinner table.

You could say the corn boat experience inspired me to pursue my culinary career, studying at the New England Culinary Institute after high school. Today, as proprietors of 1844 House, in Potsdam, my husband and I showcase corn boats, as we do all seasonal and local ingredients, during the peak of their season.

2 tbsp. butter

1 small onion, chopped

2 tsp. cumin

$^1/_2$ tsp. ground coriander

8 ears of corn cut from cob, saving the husk in one piece

$^1/_2$ lime, juiced

Dash Tabasco

$^1/_2$ cup mayonnaise

8 oz. Monterey Jack cheese, shredded

Sweat the onion, cumin and coriander in butter over low heat until the onion is translucent. Add the corn and cook over medium heat 2 to 3 minutes, or until corn is just heated through. Add lime, Tabasco and mayonnaise and stir to combine. Turn off heat and add 6 of the 8 oz. of cheese to the filling. Combine and season with salt and pepper to taste. Take the corn husk (you want it mostly intact with the exception of a few leaves peeled away to create a boat-like vessel in which to stuff the corn filling), fill each husk with corn filling and top with the remaining cheese. Bake in a 350° oven for about 20 to 30 minutes, or until heated through and cheese is golden brown. If desired, top with buttered bread crumbs or even crushed tortilla strips.

Serves 8.

Johnnycakes from Local Corn, *Mark and Kristin Kimball, Essex*

When Mark and I moved to Essex in 2003, we set out to build a farm around what we like to eat. We wanted a whole diet, one that would be satisfying, nourishing and interesting year-round. And as long as we were going to the trouble of growing for ourselves we figured we might as well grow for our neighbors, too. We began with a milk cow named Delia that first fall and by spring we'd added chickens, beef cattle and pigs. As the snow melted, we tapped the sugar bush and were rewarded with a year's worth of sweetness. We planted about 40 different kinds of vegetables and herbs, plus lots of flowers, which were strictly for morale. (Thank goodness for the flowers. That first year, we were so tired we hardly cared what we ate, but the flowers buoyed our souls.) Five years on, Essex Farm feeds 100 members who come to the farm once a week year-round to pick up their share of the harvest. We, and many of our members, live pretty much on what we grow.

One thing I've learned is that vegetables are like the covergirls of local food: sexy, flashy, visually appealing, and when it comes down to it, not too terribly handy about the place. The real heavy lifting of feeding people is done by the kind of crops that never get their pictures taken. In our region, that's wheat, field corn and the lowly, dirty potato. But here's the surprise. You can find as much subtlety and flavor in these workhorse crops as in your fanciest heirloom tomatoes. Before I started farming I'd never cooked with freshly ground cornmeal before. I thought cornmeal was supposed to taste like old cardboard. Then we grew a quarter acre of a corn called Mandan Bride. It's an antique and colorful variety, with speckled ears that range from vermilion to azure. I was so taken with the complex, nutty flavor of its meal I made johnnycakes every day for two weeks. Here's what passes for my recipe. The key is to start with cornmeal that is freshly ground—from corn grown, of course, right here in the North Country.

At Tucker Farms, corn—labeled for the curious and, well, clueless, Gabriels. Nancie Battaglia

Use about $1/2$ cup of cornmeal for every person you're feeding, and add salt to taste—a scant tsp. per cup of meal is about right. Stir in enough boiling water to make a stiff batter, about 2 cups for every cup of meal. Heat a cast-iron skillet and add a generous knob of butter. Drop the batter into rounds 3 inches across and $3/4$-inch thick. Cook on medium heat until crispy and browned, about 7 minutes per side. Eat them hot with additional butter and maple syrup for breakfast, or serve them as a side to roasted meats, topped, if you like, with a dollop of sour cream and a sprinkle of chives.

Three Sisters Salad, *George Arnold, Potsdam*

*A*s the chef for the State University of New York, Potsdam, I had many challenging menus to prepare, since the college frequently had special guests. One such group was the Mohawk chiefs from Akwesasne. I didn't want to try an authentic recipe, but I did want to honor the chiefs' heritage and make them feel welcome. I read about the legend of the Three Sisters, which explains the relationship of corn, beans and squash to each other in the culture, history and diet of the Mohawk people, and decided to build a salad around this story. The salad was very well-received and I have had many requests for the recipe.

1 qt. corn, roasted

1 qt. kidney beans, drained and rinsed

1 qt. diced zucchini

1 qt. cooked wild rice

1 cup chopped parsley

2 cups oil (walnut oil preferred)

¹/₂ cup apple cider vinegar

¹/₄ cup maple syrup

Salt and pepper, to taste

Mix corn, beans, squash, rice and parsley. In another bowl whisk vinegar into the oil. Add maple syrup, salt and pepper. Toss vegetables with dressing. Let it marinate at least 2 hours, tossing once or twice.

Serves 16 to 20.

Chef George Arnold at work in his SUNY Potsdam kitchen. Nancie Battaglia

---

Mohawk Corn Soup, *Denise White, Akwesasne*

1 large turnip

2 lbs. carrots

6 one-lb. cans of hominy

4 one-lb. cans of kidney beans

3 lbs. pork

Salt and pepper, to taste

Boil pork until tender. Remove from kettle and cut into small pieces, removing fat. Return meat to kettle. Add chopped turnips and carrots. Add hominy and kidney beans. Simmer 30 minutes. Season to taste.

Serves 30.

> **Note from Chef George:** While Mohawk Corn Soup is a tradition at Akwesasne, it doesn't fit into my vegetarian diet. If you don't eat meat, try pan-roasting fresh-cut corn, then add stock, cream, potatoes and thyme, with salt and pepper to taste.

Right: *Grabbing grilled corn in the Adirondacks.* Nancie Battaglia

Squashed by Squash, *Neal Burdick, Canton*

Last spring, with the kids grown up and gone and our backs going, my wife and I decided to downsize our garden. We went from five eight-by-eight-foot raised beds to one eight-by-24-foot plot. In it we planted mari-golds, green beans, peppers, four tomato plants, the requisite zucchini and a couple of innocent-looking butternut squash seeds in a modest hill. Add to this our perennial rhubarb and sketchy asparagus beds, and we thought we'd have a respectable and tidy village garden.

Winter squash and gourds in the North Country. Nancie Battaglia

As the summer progressed, so did our garden, more or less on schedule. The squash vines, though, were a little too enthusiastic, and we had to keep training them to wrap around this and that and trimming them back. We put up a fence to keep the deer at bay, and when the squash vines climbed the fence in an apparent sacrificial offering to the critters, we let them stay there. The deer obligingly kept them nipped back to the fence line and left everything else alone. We pretended we'd planned it that way back in raw, heartbreaking March.

Monster zucchini at Rivermede Farm, Keene Valley. Nancie Battaglia

Then we went away for a few days in August,

and when we came back, the vines had lost all sense of decorum.
They'd insinuated themselves in amongst the bean plants.
They'd ascended the pepper plants for a better view. And they'd
hauled themselves up the tomato
cages and overwhelmed the tomatoes, slapping them down with
leaves the size of tennis rackets. We
named the insidious network

A sign from the kids' community garden in Tupper Lake. Nancie Battaglia

"Audrey II" in honor of the voracious greenery in the musical
Little Shop of Horrors. We harvested what pittance from the con-
quered plants that we could, threw in the trowel and prayed for
blessed frost.

What lessons have we taken away from this? If you turn your back on butternut squash for so much as an instant, it will morph into express kudzu and grow so fast you can hear it. Never leave a garden untended in August if you hope to retain any facade of authority. If you have any sense at all, you'll swear off gardening altogether and get your veggies at your nearest farmers' market. It's cheaper, more sociable, less sweaty—and besides, those people actually know what they're doing. And how many squashes did we get out of all those miles of malicious, imperialistic vine? Three, one of which was hollow, much like my gardening skills.

Note from Chef George: The French must suffer from the classic "zucchini problem" too, as they have many recipes using zucchini or summer squash. Before you begin a recipe, trim off both ends from a cleaned squash and drop the whole zucchini into boiling salted water and cook for about 10 minutes (until flesh yields slightly). This will minimize the oozing out of the vegetable water (they are excessively watery vegetables) yet leave it not quite cooked through. As you remove the squash from the boiling water, plunge it into cold water to stop the cooking. Now it is ready for preparing in a variety of ways.

My favorite is to cut the zucchini (as prepared above) into $1/2$-inch-thick round slices. Sauté in a mixture of oil and butter until well warmed but not browned. Season with salt, pepper, chopped scallions and chopped tarragon, to taste. Add about $3/4$ cup of heavy cream and simmer about 10 minutes. Top with fresh chopped parsley.

Zucchinis Ahoy, *Lynn Case Ekfelt, Canton*

The most poignant zucchini story I ever heard came from my friend Pete, himself a gardener. He told me that his son, out on the Little River near Canton for an afternoon of fishing, had watched a flotilla of baseball-bat zucchini float by. We shared a moment of silent contemplation, considering the anguish that gardener must have felt when he realized he couldn't even *drown* them.

Left: *Nancy Bernstein, son Reuben, right, and Adrian Hayden, watering their Vermontville garden.* Nancie Battaglia

Zucchini Stuffed with Chèvre, Corn and Red Pepper, *Paul Graham, Canton*

*H*ere's how to make stuffed zucchini the long way. First, grow your own zucchini and red peppers. Our zucchini seedlings come from Miller's Greenhouse, in Lisbon. When we first visited the nursery five years ago, I had never been to Lisbon. My wife drove while I squinted at the road signs. When we finally pulled up two hours later, we saw Amish buggies and knew this was the place. We have been going to Miller's ever since.

While your zucchini grows, find a goat farm. Don and Shirley Hitchman live on County Meadows Farm, between Canton and Morley. They have a mailbox shaped like a goat. You pull up, walk into the cheese house, take what you need from the fridge (be sure to close the door tightly), and leave your money in the coffee can.

Now find some sweet corn. People sell it on the side of the road. Assemble the ingredients. By now it's probably August.

2 medium zucchini

2 tsp. olive oil or butter

2 shallots, minced

1 clove garlic

2 ears of corn cut from cob

1 small sweet red pepper, diced

4 oz. soft goat cheese

Salt, pepper and oregano, to taste

¹/₄ cup breadcrumbs

Blanch the zucchini in boiling water until firm but tender, then plunge them into cold water to stop the cooking. Meanwhile, preheat the oven to 350°. When cool, snip the ends from the squash, slice lengthwise and seed. Set aside. Sauté the shallots and garlic in olive oil (or butter) until translucent and sweet-smelling. Add the corn and the red peppers, sauté over medium heat for about 5 minutes. Turn off the heat, add the goat cheese and stir until well-blended. Season with salt, pepper and oregano. Stuff the zucchini with the mixture, top with breadcrumbs (preferably home-made) and bake for 15 to 20 minutes.

Serves 2 to 4.

Kids tend to their community garden in Tupper Lake. Nancie Battaglia

Summer squash at North Country School, Lake Placid. Nancie Battaglia

**Three Grate Ways to Use Zucchini and
Have a Perfect Summer Supper,** *Jackie Sauter, Canton*

1. SAUTÉ: Grate zucchini (or soft-skinned yellow summer squash) on the large-holed side of a metal hand-grater (or you could use the coarse-blade attachment on your food processor) into a colander. It's not a bad idea to place the colander in a bowl to catch the juices while you grate. Sprinkle grated zucchini with about a tbsp. of salt and stir. Leave the colander in the sink to drain for about 20 minutes, then rinse with water to remove excess salt and use your hands to squeeze out as much water as possible. At this point you'll have a lot less zucchini than you thought you did. Heat a few tbsp. of olive oil in a large skillet. Add zucchini and sauté. You can add grated onion, carrot, herbs, pepper, whatever. You don't need to add any more salt. Stir frequently. When the zucchini seems cooked through, top with some grated cheese and serve. Garnish with some freshly sliced garden-ripened tomatoes on the side.

2. LATKES: Grate zucchini, then salt, rinse and drain, as above. Add a couple eggs, some grated onions, chopped basil, freshly grated pepper and a tbsp. or 2 of flour. Mix. Heat a few tbsp. of oil in a skillet. Drop batter with a large spoon into the pan. Fry and flip and fry. Serve with sour cream or salsa.

3. SOUP: Coarsely grate zucchini as above, but do not salt or drain. Drop grated zucchini into a pot of chicken or vegetable broth. (Store-bought is fine.) Add a diced onion, a tbsp. or 2 of curry powder, salt and pepper, herbs of choice, maybe some chopped greens. Simmer 20 minutes or so. Serve with dollops of yogurt.

Zucchini Tomato Salad, *Yvona Fast, Lake Clear*

1 tbsp. olive oil

1 small clove garlic

$^1/_2$ tsp. salt

1 tsp. crushed basil

1 tbsp. fresh lemon juice

2 small zucchini, diced
(about 3 cups)

1 sweet onion, peeled and diced

$^1/_2$ bell pepper, diced

2 tomatoes, diced (about 3 cups)

Place the oil in bottom of salad bowl. Crush the garlic with salt, and then add to oil. Add basil, stir; whisk in lemon juice. Add the vegetables, except for the tomatoes, and stir to blend. Leave to marinate for an hour or longer. Stir in tomatoes right before serving.

Serves 8.

Ben's Blue Mountain Center Salad Dressing, *Ben Strader, Blue Mountain Lake*

Mix into blender:

$^1/_2$ cup water

$^1/_2$ cup apple-cider vinegar

$^1/_2$ cup tamari

1 $^1/_2$ cups nutritional yeast flakes (use less if powder)

1 $^1/_2$ cups safflower oil

Finely chopped garlic, to taste

Blend away, then pour on just about anything but ice cream, and enjoy.

Note from Chef George: Summer is salad season. Almost any combination of vegetables, legumes, grains, pasta and cooked meat or seafood bound together with a dressing will be satisfying. My favorites include Red, White and Blue Tomato Salad (wedges of tomatoes lightly tossed with thinly sliced sweet onions, chopped scallions and chunks of bleu cheese in an Italian vinaigrette); French-style Potato Salad (red potatoes mixed with chives, Dijon mustard, mayonnaise, garlic and chopped parsley); and Asparagus-Barley Salad (chunks of blanched asparagus, cooked and cooled barley, toasted walnuts, chopped parsley, lemon peel, lemon juice and mayonnaise).

Colorful Veggie-Stuffed Peppers, *Julie Robards, Upper Jay*

Here is my favorite summertime dinner party veggie side dish. It is so colorful and delicious, a terrific do-ahead that can be prepared hours before cooking. Not only are these peppers awesome with grilled lamb chops or beef—they make a beautiful stand-alone vegetarian meal. I can't really tell you much about the tradition of this dish except that when my husband, Terry, and I got together, we found we each had met our match—we both loved to entertain and pair good food with fine wines. I couldn't wait to start cooking for his friends—and this was one of the variations of stuffed peppers I came up with. Incidentally, it is also very good just tossed together and baked in a casserole dish or zapped in the microwave. The only way you can mess it up is to overcook it.

1 small zucchini

1 small yellow summer squash

1 Vidalia or sweet onion

1 pt. grape or sweet cherry tomatoes

6 large multicolored sweet peppers (look for peppers that have 4 lobes on the bottom so they sit evenly in the baking pan)

6 oz. feta cheese

1/2 cup good olive oil

Fresh basil, thyme and oregano, to taste

Freshly ground pepper and salt, to taste

Begin by washing and drying all vegetables and herbs thoroughly. Prepare fresh herbs by cutting up the oregano and basil leaves; remove thyme leaves from the stems. (I usually add several tbsp. of chopped herbs because I love the flavor.) Cut peppers in half, remove stems and scoop out insides. Arrange peppers in a foil-lined baking pan.

Preheat oven to 400°.

Dice zucchini, summer squash and onion into bite-sized pieces. In a large bowl combine diced vegetables with grape tomatoes, feta cheese and fresh herbs. Toss together with olive oil, and freshly ground pepper and salt.

Stuff pepper halves with the vegetable and cheese mixture, using your fingers to arrange the vegetables as compactly as possible. Vegetables will shrink during cooking so heap them up. Any remaining mixture can be baked in an ovenproof bowl and added to top off the peppers. Cover with foil, to retain shape and color, and bake for 30 minutes. Remove the foil and test for doneness. To lightly brown the peppers, pull back foil and cook for another 5 to 10 minutes. Serve with French bread to sop up pan juices, and cold, crisp white wine such as a Sauvignon Blanc or unoaked Chardonnay.

Serves 12 as a side dish.
Serves 6 as a main dish.

Savoy Salad, *Ellen Rocco, DeKalb*

Some people collect things—bottle caps, matchbooks, Depression glass, old tools. Some people go beyond collecting—they hoard, to the point of obsession. Me, I just don't care that much about "stuff." In fact, I'm the opposite—I love the feeling of throwing or giving away the things that clutter closets, shelves and cupboards. But I do have a summer obsession. I know I go way overboard. I know there's no way to use it all, I know it's perishable and visitors to my garden wonder why on earth I grow so many greens. I cannot pass a seed rack without buying another packet of Bibb lettuce or arugula or Swiss chard (both red and green, of course) or spinach (all kinds), Asian mustards and cabbages. It's a sickness, I know, worthy of a 12-step program. But after months of store-bought salad, I want to be sure I have fresh salad and cooking greens every single day from late spring through fall. I succession plant in such abundance that I cannot give the stuff away fast enough. Visit me in the summer and you don't have to worry about zucchini on the backseat of your car, but do check for the large bags of romaine and oakleaf and kale. Maybe I should raise rabbits.

Adirondack crop of Chinese cabbage.
Nancie Battaglia

Savoy salad is incredibly simple and always a hit.

1 head of Savoy cabbage or bok choy

4 green onions

2 tbsp. sesame oil (approx.)

2 tbsp. olive oil (approx.)

2 tbsp. soy sauce

1 lemon (approx.)

Salt and pepper, to taste

Very finely slice cabbage and onions and combine in a large bowl. Toss with oils (amounts are estimated based on size of cabbage used). Add and toss with soy sauce, lemon, and salt and pepper. That's it. Don't worry about making too much. I've found leftovers of this salad always get eaten the next day.

Variations: For a spicy salad, use about a $1/2$ tsp. of hot (spicy) oil or some crushed red pepper. For a different flavor, use only olive oil and add some finely chopped fresh dill to the salad. For a more traditional flavor, substitute 2 tbsp. of mayonnaise for the sesame oil, and add chunks of fresh tomato or a tbsp. of caraway seed. You see? This can go on and on.

Serves 4 to 8.

Beet and Goat Cheese Salad, *Rhonda Butler, Au Sable Forks*

We produce fresh goat cheese at Asgaard Farm, so of course I recommend our product. This recipe is easy and delicious.

4 beets about the size of your fist

5 oz. dairy-fresh chèvre (plain or flavored)

½ cup walnut pieces

Mixed garden greens

Maple vinaigrette

Maple vinaigrette:

½ cup extra virgin olive oil

¼ cup maple-flavored vinegar

1 tbsp. Dijon mustard

Salt and pepper, to taste

1 to 2 tsp. chopped fresh chives, basil, oregano and/or thyme (optional)

Combine all vinaigrette ingredients in a tightly sealed container and shake to combine.

Wrap the beets in foil and bake at 350° for 45 to 60 minutes or until they can be easily pierced with a fork. Remove the beets from the oven and cool. Gently slide the skins off beets. (Beets can be prepared 2 or 3 days ahead of time and stored in the refrigerator.)

Wash and dry the garden greens. Assemble onto 1 large plate or 4 smaller plates. Slice or dice the beets on top of the garden greens. Dot the beets and greens with pieces of fresh chèvre. Sprinkle the walnuts on top of the salad. Drizzle with maple vinaigrette, to taste.

Serves 4.

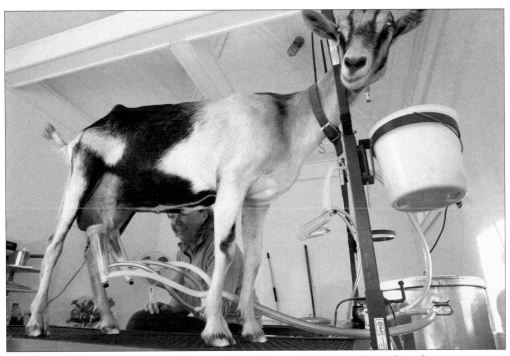

Rhonda Butler Brunner with Mazie at milking time, Asgaard Farm, Au Sable Forks. Nancie Battaglia

Fresh Garden Salsa, *Jill Rubio, Potsdam*

5 to 6 cups chopped fresh tomatoes, or a mixture of fresh tomatoes and canned chopped tomatoes (preferably Muir Glen fire-roasted)

1 to 2 jalapenos or other hot peppers

1 medium onion (sweet onions with green stems are best)

1 medium bell pepper

4 cloves garlic, minced

1 handful cilantro, minced

1 to 2 tbsp. chili powder

¹/₂ tsp. salt or pepper, to taste

Chop all vegetables, mix together with other ingredients. The heat depends on the strength of the hot peppers. If it's still not spicy enough, add a bit of cayenne. Optional: for black bean and corn salsa, add 1 cup drained, rinsed black beans and 1 medium ear of freshly steamed corn, cut off the cob.

Serves 16.

Note from Chef George: "Salsa" is Italian and Spanish for sauce. It is also the general name for hot sauces in Mexican-American cooking. I like to make a fresh corn salsa with sweet onions, hot peppers, corn, toasted pine nuts or pepitas and cilantro. It goes very well with grilled chicken.

North Country peppers. Nancie Battaglia

Summer Garden Pasta, *Carol Berard, Canton*

If you are fortunate enough to have a garden, go out and pick a handful of parsley and a handful of basil. Pull 6 or 8 green onions (scallions). Pick several small zucchini and 6 or so tomatoes, depending on size. You can use paste tomatoes or just the regular ones. By now the smell of all of these ingredients should make you pretty hungry. In the house, put on a kettle of water to boil for the pasta. Prepare the garden ingredients while the water is heating.

Chop both green and white parts of the scallions. Mince a few cloves of garlic. Dice zucchini into ¼-inch pieces. Peel and seed tomatoes and then chop them into bite-sized pieces. Rough chop parsley and basil.

In a skillet, sauté scallions in a mix of butter and olive oil until they wilt. Add the zucchini and cook till crisp-tender. Add the minced garlic and the tomatoes and simmer until most of the liquid from the tomatoes is gone. Add the parsley and basil. Simmer for about 5 minutes while the pasta is cooking.

You can use linguine or spaghetti. Of course, fresh homemade pasta is divine. To give the sauce a fresh pesto flavor, pass some toasted pine nuts and grated cheese at the table.

Mangia!

Pasta with Herbs and Raw Tomato, *Lance Myler, Potsdam*

This stuff is the soul of summer in our house. It can be ready in 20 minutes, requires no more cooking than boiling water, and tastes like a garden in the sun. We usually serve it with good bread, brushed with a bit of olive oil and toasted under the broiler. Sometimes we grate a bit of fresh mozzarella cheese over the toasted bread and briefly re-grill.

1 ½ lbs. fresh tomatoes

3 tbsp. fresh basil

1 tbsp. fresh sage

3 tbsp. fresh Italian (flat) parsley

1 tbsp. fresh rosemary

1 tbsp. fresh mint

1 lb. campanelle or some other bite-sized pasta

⅓ cup very high quality olive oil

Salt and pepper in a grinder

Wash tomatoes, cut them in half along their equators, squeeze out the seeds and gel, and dice into ½-inch cubes. Chop all the herbs. Combine with the tomatoes in a bowl big enough to hold the pasta. Cook the pasta in plenty of salted water.

When the pasta is nearly cooked, put the olive oil in a small saucepan and heat it until it starts to smoke. Pour the hot oil over the tomato-herb mixture. This is very dramatic and fun to do at the table. Add a bit of salt and several grindings of fresh pepper. Drain the pasta and toss into the sauce. Serve at once.

Serves 4 to 6.

Table Bread, *Ellen Rocco, DeKalb*

I've never regretted my decision to move to the North Country. In the summer, can you think of a better place to be? (Ditto for the rest of the year, as far as I'm concerned.) But after leaving New York City, I did miss having good bakery bread. So I learned to bake my own, going so far as to grind wheat berries—sometimes wheat that I'd grown and threshed—in a handmill attached to my kitchen counter. I'm not that ambitious anymore, though it was certainly worth the effort. Nowadays there's good bread available from a variety of local bakers, but having grown accustomed to making my own bread, I still bake about once a week. Even in the summer. The recipe will yield 4 hefty baguette loaves, or 2 loaves and 1 cookie sheet of flat bread, or 2 sheets of flat bread, or a combination of loaves, flat bread and rolls.

4 1/2 cups of warm water

3 tbsp. of dry yeast

1/3 cup sugar

4 generous tsp. of salt

1/3 cup olive oil

4 cups of whole-wheat flour

2 to 4 cups white flour

Sesame seeds, rosemary and other fresh herbs, minced garlic, etc. (all optional)

More olive oil

Coarse salt

In a large bowl, dissolve yeast in warm water and stir in sugar. After yeast bubbles, stir in salt and oil. Add whole-wheat flour and stir to mix thoroughly. Now add enough white flour to make a reasonably stiff dough that can be kneaded. Knead on a floured board for a few minutes. Oil the big bowl and turn dough into it. Cover. Let rise about an hour. Punch down.

Turn dough onto a floured surface. Knead briefly then divide into 4 pieces. For baguette-shaped loaves, roll one of the dough pieces into a long rectangle, then roll up lengthwise, pinch seam and place seam-side down in an oiled baguette pan or on a cookie sheet. Repeat with remaining dough pieces. Generously brush surface of breads with water, and repeat this several times as bread rises (about 30 minutes). When ready to bake, slash top of bread and sprinkle with sesame seeds. (For rolls, divide 1/4 of the total dough into about 8 pieces, and shape each like a mini baguette.)

For flat bread, roll 2 of the dough together into a rectangle the size of your cookie sheet. Spread on oiled cookie sheet and push outward to fit the pan. This is where you can have some fun. Lightly oil surface of flatbread, press fresh crushed rosemary or other herbs onto the surface, ditto for diced fresh garlic, or diced tomatoes, olives or anything else you like with bread. Just before baking, make indentations all over the surface with your fingertips and sprinkle with coarse salt.

Bake any of these styles in a 425° oven, in the bottom of which you've placed a large flat pan of water. For the baguettes, spray water into oven several times during baking (for crusty finish). Depending on size and shape, bake 20 to 40 minutes, or until as brown as you like your bread. Cool on racks.

Right: North Country scarecrow. Nancie Battaglia

Summer Haiku, *Diane West-Doran, Canton*

Where a house once stood
abandoned flower garden
continues to grow

Eating Outdoors, *Martha Foley, Canton*

Summers, we ate outdoors as much as possible, and if we weren't all the way outdoors, we were close. When I was a kid, in the 1950s and '60s, we spent summers at our camp on the Hudson River, between Sherman Island Dam and Feeder Dam. Technically we were in South Glens Falls, not very far from then-nascent suburbs. But the two-track, very seasonal dirt road seemed to take us far away. Camp was on a high shale bank, just downstream from the Big Boom, a historic spot where hundreds of thousands of logs driven down from the Adirondacks were held back for sorting before they were floated the final miles to the mills in Glens Falls. From the picnic table, always painted dark green, you looked straight across the river, past the stone piers that were the last local remnants of those river drives. That's where we ate, unless weather drove us onto the screened porch. Only a wind-driven rain sent us all the way inside.

We launched many a picnic cruise from camp. The Hudson there is divided into big, wide ponds by hydropower dams, so you can't go too far by boat. Perfect, though, for a slow trip upstream. Sometimes the spring flood left sandy beaches up past Big Bay. Then we'd disembark and maybe roast hot dogs. Otherwise, we'd cut the engine and eat sandwiches, riding the slow current back home.

Cookout at a Wilmington campground. Nancie Battaglia

On weekends, boat picnics took us on day trips to Lake George—a mighty undertaking, involving hauling the boat out, trailering it to Dunham's Bay, launching and seeing how far north we could go and still have time for a picnic, swim, and the trip back down the lake before dark. Not to mention the food: potato salad, macaroni salad, tomatoes to slice, pickles, chips, dips, fried chicken, hamburgers and hot dogs, brownies, marshmallows, melon, Cokes and coffee, meticulously packed into the cooler and the pack basket.

Those were picnics in paradise, but we ate outdoors in

every season. In spring we toasted our hot dogs in the arch at the sugarhouse at Madison's, on Hadley Hill. Winter we were around an open fire—hot dogs again, or peanut butter and mayonnaise sandwiches with bacon or dill pickles. No kidding. And fudge.

I still like to cook and eat outdoors. We still have meals on the porch at home in Canton, or at the picnic table at camp, a different camp now on Lake Ozonia. And we pack boat picnics, for Lake Champlain and the Thousand Islands, as well as Lake George.

Dinner transported by llama to Big Crow Mountain, Keene. Nancie Battaglia

Now the menu might include:

Pickin-up Chicken

Make this the day before a picnic, and pack lots of napkins.

Use chicken pieces—thighs and drumsticks or wings, bone-in breasts whacked in half. Prepare marinade (this is enough for one chicken or an equivalent amount of chicken drumsticks, wings or breasts):

2 to 3 cloves garlic

Fresh herbs of your choice and availability—marjoram, tarragon, thyme, oregano, basil (or dried if it isn't the season)

$1/2$ cup dried fruit (apricots are wonderful as they plump up and soften; or prunes, figs, raisins, craisins)

$1/4$ to $1/3$ cup of something salty and distinct, like olives, capers or caper berries

$1/4$ to $1/3$ cup darkish maple syrup

$1/4$ to $1/3$ cup dry vermouth

Wine vinegar and olive oil in equal parts—not too much

Salt and pepper

Marinate chicken overnight, if possible. Bake at 350° in a shallow dish for about an hour. Garnish with fresh parsley or cilantro or more of the fresh herbs. For a picnic, drain the fruit and olives and pack separately. And you *will* need napkins.

I've had versions of this recipe, called various things, in various households. It's always sensational. A tip of the hat to *The Silver Palate Cookbook*. Theirs is called Chicken Marbella. They use oregano, prunes, olives and capers, and brown sugar. And they don't add the sugar or wine to the marinade, only as the chicken goes into the oven.

Serves 4 to 6.

Fishing Up North, *Lynn Case Ekfelt, Canton [published originally in* Living North Country*]*

My husband's fishing buddy Bob earnestly assures us, "Fishing makes good sense. It fills the freezer for free." The truth is that he, like most North Country fishermen, would continue to fish even if he had to pay a surcharge on every fish he caught. In fact, a few years ago a two-week-long fishing derby was held on the St. Lawrence River in which a bass was tagged and released. Anyone catching the tagged fish within the prescribed period was to win $1 million. Sure enough, a local man caught the fish early one morning. Rather than miss out on a day of fishing, he put the fish on his stringer, went back to casting, and turned in his winner when he quit for the night.

Bullheads, *Ellen Rocco, DeKalb*

Netting the catch on Tupper Lake. Nancie Battaglia

I*n the early days of working at North Country Public Radio, I sought opportunities to speak with community groups about the station—the Masons, Elks, senior citizens' clubs, libraries. No one knew who we were or what we did. It was tricky to explain* All Things Considered *to people who were unfamiliar with public radio. In desperation, I'd say things like, "We're like public television, only on the radio." The same thing happens with bullheads. When I mention them to friends or family or people at meetings from other parts of the country, there's a blank stare and then, "What are bullheads?" I say, "They're like catfish, only much smaller—the petite northern version."*

I love bullheads. *I am essentially a vegetarian except for an occasional piece of fish or seafood. Bullheads are my favorite (except for* raw oysters). There are all kinds of bullhead feeds around the region in late spring and early summer—a great way to sample them and meet nice people. Bullheads are easy to come by if you fish—they are most plentiful in ponds and relatively slow-moving water. If a neighbor fishes and will share some with you (pre-cleaned is a real bonus in the case of bullheads), do try them. Perhaps I love bullheads because they are one of the few foods that must be fried. There is no boiling or baking or grilling. Fry them.

Here's what I do, *though everyone has their own technique. If bullheads are very small (5 to 6 inches), I cook them whole; if larger,*

I may cut them in half or at least open up the belly cavity enough to flatten them out in the pan. Combine equal amounts of flour and cornmeal in a sturdy brown paper bag, sprinkle in some salt

Sign along State Route 812 in Lewis County. Nancie Battaglia

and pepper. Beat a few eggs in a flat bowl. Dip fish in egg then toss in flour mixture. Fry in about an inch of hot vegetable oil until thoroughly cooked and nicely browned and crispy. Drain on paper. Eat hot.

Shore Dinner for Five or More, *John and Mark Scarlett, Rossie*

Beginning in the late 1940s our parents vacationed at an island cottage on Loughborough Lake, three miles by boat from Battersea, Ontario, just north of Kingston. The two of us and our sister Gwen spent our summers there. We continue to compose creative variations on the theme of a Canadian fishing guide's shore dinner learned by Dad from his friend and guide Clifford Convery. Who knows how long ago guides in Upper Canada came up with this cardio-challenging cookout, but this is a version that has migrated south to Rossie.

Gather together a convivial assortment of close friends, seasoned with family to taste. Serve your favorite libation. (Once it was Coke spiked with 151 rum, when we were young and thought we would live forever.)

In a fire circle made from dry-laid local rocks spanned by a sturdy iron grill, build a fire with nearby hardwoods cut and stacked the year before.

Above: *The Scarlett family and friends gather for a shore dinner.* Mark Scarlett, Rossie. Right: *Summer in the Adirondacks.* Nancie Battaglia

Slice clean, unpeeled homegrown potatoes approximately ¹/₈-inch thick (thick enough to be called food, rather than a snack) and place in cold water seasoned with vinegar, hot sauce and "Rossie Red" garlic to taste.

Fry 3 lbs. of thickly sliced bacon until crispy brown in a large cast-iron frying pan. (We use canola oil now, but we really did use that much bacon.) Reserve the fat in the pan, drain the bacon in a wire basket, and serve.

In the bacon fat, deep-fry whole mushrooms until brown, drain in a wire basket, dump into a brown paper bag, add salt, shake and serve in a wooden bowl with toothpicks. (Watch out. They're piping hot inside.)

Drain and add the potatoes in batches just large enough to be covered with bacon fat, heated to just below its flash point. Cook until crispy brown, with just enough meat inside to remind you that they were once lowly potatoes. (This will take years to master.) Drain in wire basket, dump into a fresh brown paper bag, add salt, shake and serve in the same wooden bowl, now empty of mushrooms.

Put breaded, freshly caught bass filets into the same bacon fat, fry and serve with tabouli, liberally seasoned with homegrown garlic, and a garden salad of local ingredients, depending on the season. (Lately, we've had good weather for shore dinners from April to November.)

If bass are out of season or you are out of luck, you may substitute homegrown chicken steeped in a savory fruit juice marinade; homegrown beef, sliced no less than 1 inch thick; or your favorite version of venison barbecue.

When everyone's back is turned and unprepared for the fireball about to erupt, pour the remaining bacon fat (canola oil) onto the fire. This will redden any faces not already crimson from the rum and Cokes, a day under ozone-depleted sunshine, or the heart-pounding calories already consumed.

Our traditional dessert is chocolate chip-peanut butter cake and ice cream (if some-one has the ambition at that point to trek to the house for the ice cream).

Invariably, the evening winds down well after dark, with a swelling chorus of bull-frogs in the distance and everyone gathered closely 'round, our bodies and souls nourished by the essential ingredients of a traditional shore dinner—good friends, good food and a crackling warm fire.

Driftwood Cod Stew, *Dr. Blair Madore, Potsdam*

I grew up on the west coast of Newfoundland and spent nearly every weekend at the family camps at Madore's Cove. My father was one of 11 children, so there was always a large collection of aunts, uncles, cousins and even a few friends present. Saturday afternoons the men would organize a group of kids to collect driftwood and build a fire on the beach. Uncle Walt would put an iron pot on top of the fire and start by frying pork fat and onions. My father would cut the potatoes and put those in. To complete the fish stew, Uncle Jerome and Uncle Norm would fill the pot with filets of fresh cod.

Rob Lamoy trolls Lake Champlain. Nancie Battaglia

While it cooked, every adult and child would find a piece of driftwood and try to whittle a wooden spoon. There was much struggling with pocketknives. The rule was that if you didn't make the spoon yourself you couldn't use it. You had to have a spoon if you wanted to eat the fish stew.

The lid was lifted and the amazing aroma drew us in. Everyone gathered around the pot and fought for their share. It tasted like the ambrosia of the gods. All too quickly the pot was empty and the precious "spoons" were added to the fire.

Paella, *John F. Schwaller, Potsdam*

I magine a hot summer day (temperatures over 100°) in the countryside of Old Castile, Spain. My wife and I happened upon a picnic ground off a secondary highway outside Valladolid and pulled off under the shade of the pine trees to eat ham-and-cheese sandwiches with our beer. We watched in amazement as family after family arrived and set up lawn chairs and picnic baskets. Then out came the cooler chests and grills, and the mamas and abuelas (grandmothers) started frying chicken. The scent of pine needles on the fires and chicken frying was heavenly enough, but then out came the longaniza sausages and even shrimp from the coolers. Lastly, the most superb meal of the summer, paella al carbón: rice permeated with the pinewood fire smoke and a little crunchy, burned against the side of the paella pan. What we would have given to have been invited to share and eat with all the rest.

2 cups chicken broth with 3 saffron threads

1 lb. chicken breasts, cut into bite-sized cubes (or one chicken cut up)

3 tbsp. olive oil

1 onion, minced

1 medium tomato, peeled, seeded and chopped

1 cup rice

8 to 10 oz. shrimp

1 cup peas

1 sprig parsley, chopped

6 oz. pepperoni, sliced (or aged chorizo)

2 cloves garlic

2 to 3 tbsp. chopped pimientos (homemade are best) or red bell peppers

1 tsp. turmeric or 3 threads saffron

1 tsp. paprika (Spanish smoked paprika is the best)

Salt and pepper

If using saffron, make an infusion with the saffron threads in the chicken stock.

Heat the frying pan and add the oil. Quickly sauté the chicken until golden on all sides. Remove to a platter. Add the onions, garlic, tomato and sauté until tender. Add the turmeric (if using) and paprika. Cook slightly. Add rice and sauté briefly to coat well. Pour on the broth, salt and pepper, to taste. Add the chicken, peas and shrimp and stir to mix well. Sprinkle with parsley. Place sliced pepperoni and pimientos in a decorative design on top. Cook over medium heat, uncovered, for 15 to 30 minutes (depending on heat and the pan), until the rice is done and liquid absorbed. You can move the pan on the burner, but do not stir. The paella pan is usually quite large, at least 12 inches in diameter.

Serves 6.

Surprise Summer Shish Kabob, *Martha Foley, Canton*

I don't know if there is a cuisine that uses fresh green coriander seeds. I'd be surprised if there isn't, but I have never run across a recipe or mention of them. I first noticed them chopping up cilantro that was going to seed. Such a fragrance, I figured they had to taste good, too. Now I make sure to harvest some seeds to freeze for later. I also crush them up to add to salads. They are quite a surprise.

For when your cilantro is going to seed and your cherry tomatoes are taking over:

Marinade: (amounts are approximate)

¼ cup good olive oil

½ cup white wine

Dash or 2 of white wine vinegar

4 cloves of garlic, smashed

Fresh green coriander seeds, crushed in a pestle

Salt and pepper

Chicken cut into in 1 ½-inch chunks

Sweet onion

Cherry tomatoes

Marinate chicken (or cubed lamb) for as long as you've got before grill time.

Skewer chicken, alternating with chunks of Vidalia or other really sweet onion and solid cherry tomatoes. I actually prefer to make separate skewers of the tomatoes, or use a grill basket for them. Slather the loaded skewers with the remaining marinade. Grill.

Serve over rice or couscous. Garnish with cilantro blossoms.

Serves 4 to 6.

Local, homegrown food on the grill in the Adirondacks. Nancie Battaglia

Julie is our point person from The Crested Hens—extraordinary potluck aficionados—of the High Peaks region. You'll find other recipes from this group of remarkable cooks elsewhere in the book.

Simple Favorites on the Grill, *Julie Robards, Upper Jay*

A bundle of asparagus or green beans wrapped in a slice of bacon, drizzled with olive oil and roasted. Roasted stuffed red or yellow pepper filled with seasonal summer squash and grape tomatoes, onions, fresh thyme, feta cheese and drizzled with olive oil. We love to cook with fresh seasonal vegetables—what could be better in the summer with a crisp fruity white wine? I do a lot of vegetables on the grill—just drizzle with good olive oil.

Provisions at Hoss's Country Store, Long Lake. Nancie Battaglia

Pie eating contest, Gore Mountain. Nancie Battaglia

What to Do When the Fridge Finally Shivers, Shudders and Dies, *Dale Hobson, Potsdam*

Cool all your beer in a stream.

Pour contents of one bottle down neck.

Repeat until hungry.

Eat everything.

Barn Raising ... and Switzel, *Carol Pearsall, Johnsburg*

Barn raising conjures up visions of a community working together, each person responsible for a task, from the coordinator of the building to the middle-sized children taking care of the youngest children. I asked my cousin Ben and neighbor Earl Allen about barn raising thinking they were scheduled events in the farming year, but that was not the case. Barn raisings occurred because of need. If a neighbor's barn was destroyed, plans were set in motion to rebuild as soon as possible. If it was a new barn, plans might be done at a more leisurely pace. Still, planning was important. Just as location, materials and design were important to the barn, food was important for the workers. Records from the Town of Johnsburg Historical Society list food for 175 men for a barn raising. According to Ben, by the time the men, women and all their children were gathered it was not unusual to have 200 people to feed. It must have been a sight to see—not only the barn going up, but the tables groaning under the weight of all the food.

Great-grandmother's Recipe for a Barn Raising *(from The Town of Johnsburg Historical Society records)*

115 lemon pies

500 fat cakes (donuts)

15 large cakes

3 gallons applesauce

3 gallons rice pudding

3 gallons cornstarch pudding

16 chickens

3 hams

50 lbs. roast beef

300 light rolls

16 loaves bread

Red beet pickle and pickled eggs

Cucumber pickle

6 lbs. dried prunes, stewed

1 large crock stewed raisins

5-gallon stone jar of white potatoes and same amount of sweet potatoes

Serves 175 men.

Dairy farmer Leonhard Wiegandt and his ladies, Rensselaer Falls.
Nancie Battaglia

There was no mention of beverage, although boiled coffee and switzel were no doubt on the list. Switzel was an easy concoction to put together, its bonus being a small amount was thirst quenching—an important consideration for long days of arduous labor. At Bakers Mills Day in 2005, Jane Nevins served three different mixes of Switzel. Here are two (plus the editors have added one from St. Lawrence County):

Switzel

To one gallon of water add 2 cups of sugar, 1 cup apple cider vinegar and 2 tbsp. ginger. Mix well.

Reverend Daisy Allen's Switzel

1 gal. water

1 cup sugar

³/₄ cup vinegar

4 tsp. of ginger (depends on your taste)

Mix together in a gallon jug and keep cold.

Switchel, *Mary-Ann Cateforis, Potsdam*

Old-timers used this drink as a thirst quencher during the hot summer months. Farmers would carry a gallon jug of switchel when they went out to work in the fields. This recipe is from my old farmer friend Stanley Northrop, of Potsdam.

4 tbsp. brown sugar

Ginger, the size of a lima bean

4 tbsp. (cider) vinegar

Water to make a qt.

> **Note from Chef George:** Ginger has been used as a medicine since ancient times and is recorded in early Sanskrit, Chinese, Ancient Greek, Roman and Arabic texts. It is often credited with reducing swelling and pain in the joints.

Michigan Sauce, *Niki Kourofsky, Keene*

*H*ave you ever tried to order a michigan anywhere else in the country? I did—once. Until I moved away to college, I had no idea that the rest of America was missing out on the North Country's favorite meat condiment. My late-night order was met with a blank stare, and attempts to explain only resulted in more confusion, punctuated by grumbles from the growing line behind me. Finally the cook yelled from the kitchen, "Why doesn't she just order a chili dog?" Humph. Chili dog? I think not.

Everyone in the North Country has an opinion about michigans: whose is the best, whose was the first, why something that can only be found in the northeast corner of New York would be called a michigan. The question is still open for debate, but according to Press-Republican columnist Gordie Little, Garth and Eula Otis, formerly of Michigan, opened Plattsburgh's first michigan stand in 1925. Mrs. Otis was a close friend of Clare, of Clare & Carl's fame (see photo below), who came up with her own version of the sauce in the 1940s.

A friend gave me the basics for this michigan sauce recipe, assuring me that it was the Clare & Carl's recipe. But just as every old-timer in the Adirondacks claims an association with Noah Rondeau, every family in Clinton County claims to have the original Clare & Carl's recipe. (If, on the off chance that this is the secret recipe, my apologies to Clare.) My version has evolved over the years to include less traditional—but very North Country—ingredients like leeks, horseradish and beer.

2 lbs. uncooked hamburger

16 oz. tomato sauce

8 to 10 tsp. chili powder

2 tsp. cumin

2 tsp. black pepper

Onion or wild leeks

2 cloves garlic (omit if using leeks)

Hot sauce, to taste (about ¹/₄ bottle)

Ketchup, to taste (makes it sweeter)

Mustard, to taste

Horseradish, to taste

¹/₄ bottle beer or less (overdoing the beer will ruin consistency)

Combine all ingredients. Cook over low heat for 2 to 3 hours.

NCPR production manager Joel Hurd's lunch—on a field trip to Plattsburgh to record a Very Special Places *feature. This perfect meal of michigans, fries and onion rings was served at Clare & Carl's, a special place on Route 9—one of the first michigan stands.*
Varick Chittenden, Canton

Dinner Al Fresco, Dinner All Local, *Elizabeth Folwell, Blue Mountain Lake (excerpted from Adirondack Life, Special Saratoga Section, August 2008)*

The old courthouse, the color of Dijon mustard in the late-day sun, stood guard over several long white tents and throngs of guests. Near a stage platform were round tables abundant with cheese made of sheep, goat and cow's milk from half a dozen creameries, plus baskets of crusty bread supplied by three bakeries.

Arrangements of cucumbers, carrots, pear tomatoes, green and yellow beans, peppers and summer squash were so meticulously displayed they looked for a moment like wedding reception centerpieces or the cover of a designer seed catalog. But this was, after all, a gala meal celebrating country fare—art is

Essex Farms produce sorters, Essex. Nancie Battaglia

transitory, at least as far as food is concerned. Every crumb, every morsel vanished. Slabs of bread, slivers of cheese, blue-ribbon vegetables disappeared as guests savored the annual event, the Salem Al Fresco Dinner.

You can't get much closer to the roots of a meal than this Washington County setting. The lawn gave way to a lush cornfield, and a hillside pasture sloped upward in another direction. Midway through the salad course a herd of dairy

Loaves from Crown Point Bread bakery offered at Lake Placid farmers' market. Nancie Battaglia

cows made their deliberate march back to the barn. Ed Yowell, head of the New York City Slow Food Group, commented, "It's about 16 miles from farm to fork here."

Since it began in 2002, the dinner has focused on agriculture and community, honoring and sustaining both. Proceeds fund historic preservation and cultur-

Cows at Clover Mead Farm, Keeseville. Nancie Battaglia

al programs at the former courthouse, now an arts center with pottery and quilting studios and a professional kitchen available for creating condiments in a health department–certified space. The Saturday night and following day are party, farm showcase, cooking school and lesson in community organizing combined. There's dancing, music—lots of music, from blues to Broadway tunes, auctions of the live and silent varieties, plus appearances by entertainers and politicians.

Annette Nielsen's vision of recreating a Tuscan outdoor supper just south of the Adirondacks, where pastures are plentiful but vineyards are not, came from a meal she shared several years ago with friends in Siena, Italy. The memory lingered, and since she calls her neighborhood the Tuscany of upstate New York, she saw how such a culinary undertaking could work. Work, though, is the key. In 2006 she got 200 pounds of local tomatoes to sun-dry herself, which translated to 10 pounds for the artisan luganega sausage made by a Shushan butcher from a traditional Italian recipe.

Though she grew up in Northville, Nielsen's life and careers have led to many places. She worked on Capitol Hill for Senator Ted Kennedy and for a gourmet caterer in New York City. In June 2001 she and her family settled in Salem, a postcard-perfect village with tree-shaded streets. Close by town are thriving farms, from long-time homesteads to new organic growers eager to be close to appreciative markets. Though she is definitely the dinner's impresario, Nielsen gives credit where it's due, to the dozens of farms, a hard-working board and "nearly 200 volunteers who make this event happen now. People set up tents and tables, pick up the food at the farms, prep, cook, clean up, serve, even make the platters and bowls for serving—they're all made at the courthouse pottery studio by volunteers."

Four hundred people attended Al

Fresco last year, spending $35 each for the best kind of cuisine, highlighting the flavors of the day's—and region's—harvest. Washington and Saratoga County farms and producers supplied everything from garlic and scallions to chicken breasts and goat-milk yogurt; only a handful of ingredients and beverages weren't local, like olive oil and coffee. Mesclun greens with raspberry vinaigrette; heirloom potato salad in shades of red, white and blue; roasted vegetables garnished with feta cheese;

Cheesemaker Sam Hendren, of Clover Mead Farm, in Keeseville, in a still taken from the film Three Farms, *by Ben Stechschulte. The film was commissioned by Adirondack Harvest.* Ben Stechschulte, Keene Valley

caramelized onion and squash torte with cornmeal crust; basil and garlic artisan sausage; aromatic herb-marinated free-range chicken; rhubarb/strawberry/apple cobbler topped with blueberries and a side of whipped cream came to the tables via local high schoolers balancing huge trays. Each tent was just one table wide, so talking to strangers was easy and natural: we all shared abiding interest in honest food done right.

Seated across from us, some of the 28 New York City slow foodies were in locavore heaven. They had come for the whole weekend, for the dinner and to tour farms on Sunday and taste the on-the-spot creations of numerous regional chefs. "When we members of Slow Food describe something—an event, a food, a producer—that is particularly aligned with our mission, to achieve a good, clean and fair food chain—where good means real food, clean means good food provided sustainably and humanely, and fair means that producers are compensated fairly and that eaters have fair access to good, clean food—we say it is 'slow,'" Yowell told us. "And Al Fresco is *slow*, a convivial gathering of producers and eaters celebrating community and enjoying local bounty."

Offerings at Essex Farm, Essex.
Nancie Battaglia

"In 2007 we sourced the dinner from 35 farmers and producers," Nielsen said. "We pay the farmers and others fair price for what they provide, and when all was said and done, the event made more than $20,000." In a barn next to the courthouse, bidders scribbled what they'd gladly pay for a perfect pie or a load of firewood; during the live auction, a set of Telescope outdoor furniture brought in big bucks. Sipping sparkling cider from a nearby orchard, sated diners watched as others danced to the raucous Roadhouse Blues Band and swayed to ballads sung by sisters Zipporah and Sarah Galimore.

The Al Fresco events take place during the last weekend in July, with tickets going on sale in early June. www.salemcourthouse.org

Nana's Strawberry Shortcake, *Sandy Demarest, Potsdam*

*I*grew up in a large, blue-collar family in rural northern New York. When summer arrived and wild strawberries were bursting, my five sisters and I would head out with little buckets to our favorite gathering spot—the base of a lone tree in the lower-back meadow. Sometimes we couldn't even tell if we were headed in the right direction because we couldn't see over the tall grasses. So we held hands and found our way together. At the end of the pilgrimage, we returned home with stained fingers and just enough berries to mix with sugar or scatter on our cornflakes. I learned this recipe from "Nana" Gray, of Maine.

4 cups flour

³/₄ cup shortening

1 tsp. salt

¹/₃ cup sugar

3 tbsp. baking powder

1 pt. milk

Preheat oven to 500°.

Sift together dry ingredients, cut in shortening until it looks like course meal. Make a well, pour in milk all at once. Stir with a fork. Turn out on a lightly floured surface and knead. Pat down and cut biscuits with a cookie cutter. Bake at 500° for the first few minutes, until they pop. Reduce temperature to 450°. Cooking time: 8 to 10 minutes. For Nana's Biscuits: omit the sugar and reduce the shortening by ¹/₄ cup.

Serves 18 to 20.

Wild Strawberries, *Meredith Mayne, Massena*

As a small girl, there was a field near my house on Wellesley Island, on the St. Lawrence River, that I would creep through in the summer, legs bare, spittle bugs smearing on my skin, on the hunt for my secret summer treat—teeny, tiny, juicy, heart-shaped, wild strawberries, perfect for small hands and mouths. The strawberries could never fill up my stomach, and the thrill of feeding myself from the earth kept me always searching for one more, just one more.

Recently I went back, longing for a pea-sized strawberry or two, only to find my field now kept shorn, my memories mowed down and mulched—just a few hearty, sneaky plants around the edges, these renegade strawberries almost, but not quite, too small to taste.

Warranted Canned Strawberries, *Diane Romlein, Potsdam*

Put 4 lbs. white sugar in a kettle, add a teacup cold water, let boil till perfectly clear. Add 4 qt. nice berries. Boil 10 minutes, keeping them covered with syrup, but avoid stirring in order to preserve their good appearance. Take out berries with a small strainer or skimmer, place in jars and let the syrup boil 10 minutes longer, then pour it over the berries when cool, putting a tbsp. of good brandy on top of each jar.

This method is the only means of preserving the peculiar flavor of the strawberries. This does make an excellent syrup for pancakes, yogurt, etc. Use a modern canning method to seal jars, or this can be frozen.

> **Note from Chef George:** The term "warranted" is used in a recipe for strawberries in an 1883 cookbook titled *Practical Housekeeping: A Careful Compilation of Tried and Approved Recipes* by Estelle Woods Wilcox. I have never seen it used otherwise in a recipe.

Fresh picked strawberries, Peru. Nancie Battaglia

Strawberry Pie, *Diane Romlein, Potsdam*

*T*hough most of our 125 acres is wetlands and woods, we garden as much of it as we can. Adam and Daniel, the youngest of our five children, love to garden and care for plants. This is part of their proud strawberry harvest from the family garden. It looks the way kids like birthday cakes to look—messy and gooey.

9-inch pie crust:

2 cups flour

Sprinkle of salt

¹/₂ cup oil

¹/₄ cup milk

Filling:

4 cups fresh berries, washed and hulled

3 tbsp. cornstarch

1 cup sugar

¹/₂ tsp. baking powder

3 drops red food coloring

Mix crust ingredients gently; roll out between sheets of wax paper. Bake crust for 15 minutes at 400°.

Spread 2 cups berries over bottom of pie shell. Mash or cut up remaining berries. Add sugar, cornstarch and baking powder; mix well. Place over low heat, bring to boil slowly, reduce heat and cool, stirring constantly. Add food coloring. Then pour over raw berries in shell. Refrigerate until thoroughly chilled. Garnish with sweetened sour cream or whipped cream.

Serves 6.

Breakfast Blueberry Cake, *Nancy Howard, Tupper Lake*

I did my very first blueberry walk with my mother-in-law, Ruth Howard, on Mount Tremblant. We had a dreamy view of the world atop, but I soon learned that blueberry picking was serious stuff.

1 cup sugar

¹/₄ cup butter

1 egg

1 cup milk

2 cups flour

Salt

4 tsp. baking powder

1 ¹/₂ cups wild blueberries

Cream butter and sugar well; add egg. Combine flour, salt and baking powder. Add alternately flour mixture and milk. Beat well. Gently flour berries and fold in lightly. Bake at 375° in a 9-by-13-inch pan and cut in squares. Serve often.

Serves 8.

Camping Blueberry Pancakes, *John and Liz Scarlett, Mark and Louise Scarlett, Rossie*

To experience this gustatory treasure in the middle of a two-week canoe trip in August is to taste the universe in a Sierra cup.

Ingredients per person:

1 cup flour (makes 3 7-inch pancakes). No more than 50 percent white flour. We often use multigrain flour or a never-duplicated mix of such flours as whole wheat, oat, buckwheat, corn, rice and bean.

1 tsp. baking powder

1 cup powdered milk (add the powder to the dry ingredients)

1 egg (one of the few luxuries)

¹/₂ cup blueberries

Water (however much for the consistency you like)

Blueberry pancakes on a camping trip. Mark Scarlett, Rossie

Remember, pancakes are idiot-proof, merely inflated and dolled up tortillas.

Into a pot empty the plastic bag that contains all the dry ingredients packaged together before the trip, add the egg, and enough water to make the batter as thick or thin as you prefer. Finally, add the blueberries you picked a few minutes ago. If you brought dried blueberries, they will already be in the bag of dry ingredients unless you choose to package them separately and reconstitute in water before adding to the batter. How many? Perhaps you could add too many, but that would be a new experience for us.

Put a few slices of precooked, vacuum-packed bacon (requires no refrigeration) and some canola oil on a frying pan or cookie sheet and pour on some batter. If you then discover, as once happened to us, that you forgot to pack a spatula, grab a hatchet and knife and madly whittle one from a dead piece of softwood. No maple syrup? We still tell the story of a trip in 1963 when we made do with a mix of brandy and brown sugar on a sub-freezing morning.

With unwavering attention and determination, the last batch, which is reserved for the cook, will finally be perfect—crispy on the outside and cooked all the way through. And if while transferring a pancake from pan to plate, you drop one on the ground, curse not, for it too belongs to the cook in all its enhanced flavor. The butter? If careful, it can survive a long summer trip. We don't bring it anymore. But we do provide a ¹/₂ cup of our own maple syrup per person per pancake meal. On our trips pancakes are both a breakfast and dinner item depending on how quickly we want to break camp.

Birthday Waffles, *Robin Rhodes-Crowell, Pierrepont*

*M*y daughter ended up being a surprise home-birth on an early September morning in *2003. She came into this world quicker than expected, and I delivered her in our wonderful old circa 1860 farmhouse. A midwife, my mother, a friend and my husband were all there, and all went well—just fast. After the excitement died down, my husband made the birth team homemade waffles. After all the energy I used in labor and giving birth, it had to be the best waffle I have ever eaten. Now my daughter always requests waffles for breakfast on her birthday and the re-telling of her birth story.*

About 1 ²/₃ cups whole-wheat pastry flour

2 tsp. baking powder

¹/₂ tsp. salt

1 tbsp. brown sugar

3 eggs, yolks and whites separated

4 tbsp. melted butter

1 ¹/₂ cups milk

Sift whole-wheat pastry flour with the baking powder, salt and sugar. In another bowl, beat the egg yolks well and then add the melted butter and milk into this same bowl. Pour the liquid ingredients into the sifted ingredients and combine but do not over-mix. Beat the egg whites until stiff. My husband says it is very important you *fold*, not stir, the egg whites in. Serve with pure maple syrup. Now, as part of my daughter's birthday breakfasts, we thaw strawberries and heat them gently in a pot until somewhat sauce-like to add to the top of the waffles.

Berries and plums at farm stand in the Adirondacks. Nancie Battaglia

Blueberry Buckle, *Peg Kelsey Cornwell, Tupper Lake summer resident*

I have discovered an amazing spot on the top of a small bald Adirondack peak near our summer camp to pick wild blueberries. For a perfect summer outing, I ride my bike to the bottom of the hill and hike up with berry-picking containers in hand. If I time it right, the top is covered with a sea of blue. I pick like crazy, trek back down and ride home. Then I sit on the porch in the sun and sift out the chaff from the blues and put them in a prominent place for all to admire.

My mother has this recipe written on a piece of scrap paper taped inside a cabinet door that holds the essential ingredients for what we call blueberry buckle (though I know by definition a blueberry buckle has blueberries in the dish—this has blueberries on the bottom). Around eight o'clock, when we are starting to think about dinner after a long day on the lake, the buckle goes in the oven and comes out warm in time for dessert. If there's any left over, the first person up in the morning inevitably decides it is prime breakfast material.

1 cup flour

³/₄ cup sugar

1 tsp. baking powder

³/₄ tsp. salt

1 egg

2 cups wild blueberries

¹/₃ cup butter

2 tbsp. brown sugar

1 tsp. cinnamon

Grease an 8-by-8-inch baking pan. Pour 2 cups of blueberries in the bottom (the more the better, of course). Mix the egg and dry ingredients together and add on top of the blues. Melt the butter, add the brown sugar. Pour over the flour mixture, sprinkle on the cinnamon. Bake at 350° for 30 minutes. Serve with ice cream, or not.

Serves 6.

Peg with a bowl of her favorite fruit, Tupper Lake.
Photographer unknown

Raspberry Cake with Raspberry Sauce, *Evelyn Greene, North Creek*

*I*n the early 1950s my mother, two sisters and a brother were climbing the 46 highest peaks in the Adirondacks. My father would often drive us north from North Creek on a Sunday afternoon and pick us up the next Saturday. We had to survive as well as we could on the food that kids and a middle-aged woman could manage to carry in or scrounge. Because we were camping in the summer, we could sometimes glean wild berries. At Lake Colden we borrowed the ranger's reflector oven and made this cake with hot raspberry sauce poured over it (which helped disguise the burned and raw bits).

Cake:

4 tbsp. shortening

¹/₂ cup sugar

1 egg (dried, rehydrated)

1 ³/₄ cups flour

2 ¹/₂ tsp. baking powder

³/₄ cup milk (dried, rehydrated)

1 cup raspberries

Cream together shortening and sugar; beat in the egg. In another bowl, sift together the flour and baking powder. Alternately mix the flour and milk into the shortening-sugar mixture. Beat until smooth. Mix in raspberries. Bake in a greased pan at 350° for about 20 to 30 minutes.

Sauce:

1 tbsp. cornstarch

¹/₂ cup sugar

Pinch of salt

¹/₂ cup hot water

2 tbsp. lemon juice

¹/₂ cup raspberries

Stir the first 3 ingredients together and mix with a little cold water. Add hot water and lemon juice, cook until clear, stirring. Add ¹/₂ cup raspberries. Pour sauce over cake while warm.

Serves 8.

Simple pleasures on Main Street, Essex.
Nancie Battaglia

Schweizer Rice, *Elise Widlund, North River*

Schweizer *means "Swiss" in German. This recipe, basically a cold rice dessert, convinced my husband that we should make our lives together.*

4 cups cooked rice (any flavor or type is fine)

1 ¹/₂ cups heavy cream

1 ¹/₂ tbsp. sugar

¹/₂ tsp. vanilla

Rice should be precooked to the slightly dry side and cold. In another chilled bowl, beat cream with sugar, adding vanilla after it begins to thicken. Fold rice into the beaten sweet cream. Serve in bowls with maple syrup.

Serves 6 to 8.

Chocolate Zucchini Cake, *Anne Burnham, Parishville*

I *call this Chocolate Zucchini Cake à la Lamar Bliss, in honor of a former North Country Public Radio staffer.*

¹/₂ cup solid shortening (margarine or Crisco)

¹/₂ cup vegetable oil

1 ³/₄ cups sugar

2 eggs

1 tsp. vanilla

¹/₂ cup buttermilk

2 ¹/₂ cups flour

¹/₂ tsp. baking powder

¹/₂ tsp. baking soda

4 tbsp. cocoa powder

¹/₂ tsp. cloves, ground

¹/₂ tsp. cinnamon

2 cups zucchini, diced

¹/₄ cup chocolate chips

Cream together the solid shortening, the oil and the sugar. Mix in eggs, vanilla and buttermilk. In another bowl sift together the flour, baking powder, baking soda, cocoa and spices. Beat this in with the first mixture. Add zucchini and chocolate chips. Put in a greased and floured 2-inches-deep, 9-by-12-inch pan and bake at 325° until done, about 40 to 45 minutes.

Serves 8.

Eggs in the southern Adirondacks. Nancie Battaglia

Magic Cookies, *Lesley Morse, Copenhagen*

Summer at Lake Bonaparte, in the northern corner of Lewis County, reminds me of Aunt Leah's Magic Cookies, a round, flavorful cookie sprinkled with sugar and topped with exactly three raisins in the center. The "magic" of these cookies was that they always appeared when you were sick, and they always made you feel better. Maybe it was just the love and care that Aunt Leah put into making them, but our entire family believes in the magic. When my sister and her four-year-old son were in a head-on collision and hospitalized with life-threatening injuries for several weeks, one of my sister's first comments was, "We need magic cookies really bad." And Aunt Leah came through once again.

2 cups sugar

1 cup shortening

3 eggs

1 tsp. vanilla

1 cup buttermilk

4 cups flour

2 tsp. baking powder

1 tsp. baking soda

$^1/_4$ tsp. salt

Cream together sugar and butter. Beat in eggs and vanilla. In another bowl sift together flour, salt, baking soda and baking powder. Alternately blend dry ingredients then buttermilk into the butter-sugar-eggs-vanilla mixture.

Cool in the refrigerator for several hours or overnight. Lightly flour board or counter and pour out some of the cookie dough; gently knead and then roll out dough to $^1/_3$-inch. Cut out round cookies about 3 inches in diameter, place on baking sheet, sprinkle with white sugar and place 3 raisins in the center. Bake at 375° for 8 to 10 minutes.

Makes 3 $^1/_2$ dozen.

Helen Straight's Ice Cream, *Recipe thanks to Carol Pearsall, Johnsburg*

Milda Donahue Burns passed along this recipe that was given to her mother-in-law, Mable Burns, by Helen (Mrs. Ben) Straight. The Straights ran the 13th Lake Lodge in North River, in the 1930s. Mrs. Straight wrote to Mrs. Burns, "I hope you enjoy this recipe."

$^3/_4$ cup flour

3 $^1/_2$ cups sugar

$^1/_2$ tbsp. salt

4 eggs

2 qt. heated milk (Blood hot!)

$^1/_4$ cup vanilla

1 pt. whipped cream

Mix flour, sugar and salt together; gradually add to heated milk. Take off stove when mixing. Add well-beaten eggs. Cook until the mixture coats a spoon! Use a double boiler! Cool, add vanilla. Strain into a freezer and hastily add 1 pt. whipped cream, and freeze!

[Carol's note: This recipe arrived with all those exclamation marks!]

Right: Sharing ice cream, Donnelly's Ice Cream, Saranac Lake. Nancie Battaglia

Small Farms, *Ellen Rocco, DeKalb*

I*f you go to the children's section in a bookstore or to any toy store, you'll find all kinds of farm stories—like* Charlotte's Web*—and toys, from three-dimensional barnyard scenes to puzzles and bags of miniature farm animals. These are always based on what, until recently, was increasingly becoming a fantasy farm rather than a real agricultural operation—namely, The Family Farm. As agriculture has consolidated in the past three or four decades, family farms largely disappeared: 50-cow dairies replaced by 500- or 1,500-head dairies; vegetable-truck farming replaced by 1,000-acre single-crop growers, often thousands of miles away. With renewed interest in locally grown food, the agribusiness trend is starting to find fledgling competition from a new generation of family farms. Often these operations provide only a portion of the household income, but it's a promising start. Among the exciting new farm products from small producers are a variety of cheeses, including chèvre (goat cheese), which is featured in two recipes from Asgaard Farm in Au Sable Forks, owned and operated by Rhonda Butler, David Brunner and their daughter Johanna. The beet and goat cheese salad recipe you'll find elsewhere in the summer section. Here's the recipe for a lovely goat-cheese cake, which Rhonda describes as "lighter than your typical cheesecake."*

Goat-Cheese Cake, *Rhonda Butler, Au Sable Forks*

Crust:

³/₄ cup coarsely ground walnuts

³/₄ cup finely crushed graham crackers

3 tbsp. melted, unsalted butter

Thoroughly combine all three ingredients. Press compactly into the bottom of a lightly buttered 9- or 10-inch springform pan.

Filling:

32 oz. Asgaard Dairy fresh, unflavored chèvre

4 large eggs

1 ¹/₄ cups sugar

1 tbsp. fresh lemon juice

2 tsp. vanilla extract

2 tbsp. unbleached, all-purpose flour

Pinch of salt

Preheat the oven to 350°.

Beat the cream cheese in a large bowl until smooth. Add the sugar, lemon juice and vanilla and mix well. Beat in the flour and salt. Add the eggs one at a time, beating well after each and stopping occasionally to scrape down the sides of the bowl. Pour the batter evenly over the crust. Bake approximately 55 minutes (45 minutes if using a 10-inch pan) or until the outer edge of the cake is puffed (and maybe a little cracked), the center is set and the top is brown in spots. Remove the cake from the oven and let cool for 15 minutes. (The top of the cake will gradually even back out and the cracks will diminish.) Keep the oven at 350°.

Topping:

2 cups sour cream

¹/₄ cup sugar

1 tsp. vanilla extract

Whisk the sour cream, sugar and vanilla together to blend. Spoon the mixture over the cake, starting at the center and extending to within ¹/₂-inch from the edge. Return the cake to the oven and bake 5 minutes longer. Remove the cake from the oven, let cool, then cover and refrigerate for at least 12 hours. For best results, leave the cake in the refrigerator for 1 to 2 days.

Before serving, remove the sides from the springform pan. Top the cake with raspberries, strawberries, blueberries or any other fresh, seasonal fruit.

Serves 10 to 12.

Autumn

As fall approaches, the garden that produced a trickle in spring and a steady supply in summer becomes an avalanche—megatons of tomato and cuke, cairns of cabbage, pecks of peppers, pyramids of potatoes. Like Lucille Ball at the assembly line, even the most voracious appetite could never keep up. After stocking the larders of friends and family and delivering loads to the food pantry, after the involuntary contributions to rabbit and deer, still the kitchen table groans beneath the load.

The feckless hedonism of summer is past; it's time to roll up the sleeves and put by for winter. Blanch it, boil it, make sauce, dry it, salt it, brine it, freeze it, can it. Squeeze out the last goodness, the way you press the windfall apples for cider. In a good year, you might eke it out all the way through the snows.

As the nights begin to frost, nothing is left at the farmstands but gourd and root. A night comes when even black plastic will not suffice to stretch the season one more day, and leaves you to watch the snow out the window, to reread the seed catalogs, and to plan the spring campaign. —**Dale Hobson**

Left: *Truckload of pumpkins for sale along the railroad tracks, Saranac Lake.*
Nancie Battaglia

The Harvest, *Ellen Rocco, DeKalb*

In late summer and early fall every gardener is tracking the weather for the first frost. In my early years of gardening I'd marshal all the tarps and old sheets I could find to cover late-fruiting peppers and tomatoes. These days I confess to welcoming the end of the growing season—enough already, let's hunker in for winter. Rather than covering plants, I harvest. Piles of tomatoes and peppers of all colors, squash, potatoes, onions and garlic fill my porch. I'll get to them, find long-term storage. First, though, I pick as many basil leaves as possible, rinse and dry them, then make tight little packages in pesto-size batches that I store in the freezer. Some people combine basil, garlic and nuts and freeze this mixture, to which cheese is added at the time the pesto is to be used. I haven't got enough time in the fall for all of this, and I've found that assembling the pesto during the winter, using the frozen leaves, is about as close to fresh pesto as I can get without buying tiny bunches of basil shipped from very far away.

Rhonda Butler Brunner picking herbs at Asgaard Farm, Au Sable Forks. Nancie Battaglia

Herbs in the Adirondacks. Nancie Battaglia

OK, my neighbor Aldena didn't teach me how to make pesto—I doubt she'd ever heard of it—but she did teach me about autumn priorities—what does and doesn't have to be done immediately, and in what order. When I hear about possible frost, the basil leaves come in.

Here's how I do winter pesto: *On 12 inch-long pieces of aluminum foil, pile as much basil (leaves only) as you can fit. Squish the basil down and wrap tightly with the foil. Freeze immediately. Fast forward to winter. In a food processor, combine a $^1/_4$ to a $^1/_2$ cup of olive oil, a package of the frozen basil leaves, $^1/_2$ cup of nuts (pine or walnut are best), fresh garlic cloves to taste (I use a whole bulb because I am convinced garlic is the most important flavor in the world), a bit of dried hot pepper and salt to taste. Process just to mix and break up large chunks, but not to the point of smooth paste. (Or, better yet, take the time to use a mortar and pestle to work up the pesto.) Put mixture in a bowl and stir in grated cheese to taste.*

Discovering Pepian Verde, *Christopher Shaw, Bristol VT*

Y ou can always discover new ways in which geographies mirror each other. In 1992 I drove from Lake Placid to Chiapas and Guatemala with the photographer Nathan Farb as part of the research for my book *Sacred Monkey River*. In Palenque, we rendezvoused with Victor Perera, the Guatemalan journalist whom I had met in Blue Mountain Lake. From Palenque, the three of us drove to San Cristobal de Las Casas, the colonial city in the Chiapas highlands. Every night the food got better: tamales, chiles rellenos and a wonderful smoky black mole in a classy *tipica* restaurant.

Mesoamerica, that geographical and cultural stretch of the Central American isthmus from Oaxaca to Honduras, is a region of forest, river, lake and mountain laced with agricultural valleys and dotted with small cities and villages, where canoes are the traditional watercraft. Sort of like the Adirondacks and the St. Lawrence and Champlain Valleys, in other words, except warmer—a kinship I felt on my first visit with Victor in 1989.

Its continuous 5,000-year-old culture is as old as China's, and it boasts a traditional cuisine that ranks with China, Italy and Vietnam as among the world's greatest, combining colonial Spanish and pre-conquest Native American elements. This is not the nachos and burritos of strip mall Tex-Mex. After my first visit in 1989, I learned to make enchiladas and huevos rancheros, but I realized after our three days in San Cristobal in 1992 how historically layered the cooking was, with many dishes deriving from before the conquest.

From San Cristobal, Nathan, Victor and I crossed the Guatemalan border at Ciudad Cuauhtemoc, a chaotic third-world entry point, en route to Victor's birthplace in Antigua. Passing our first Guatemalan army checkpoint—this was before the Peace of 1996 that ended 40 years of civil war and right-wing atrocity—Victor yelled, "Keep going!" when the soldiers waved us toward them to be checked. The highway soon entered the vertiginous canyons of the Cuchumatan Mountains, with cold clear rivers plunging north

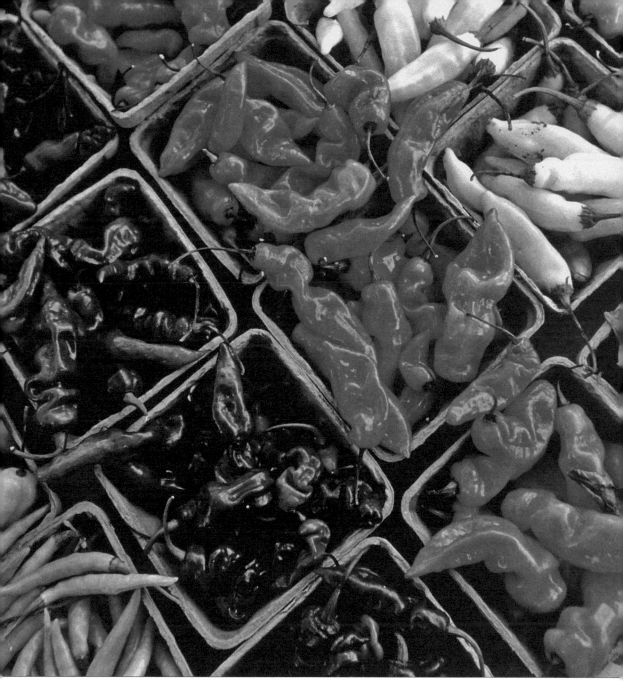

Peppers in the Adirondacks. Nancie Battaglia

through the shadows toward the Rio Suchiate and fields of maize and wheat planted on sun-splashed, near-vertical slopes high above. Everywhere traditional Mayan families came down steep trails to the road to sell their produce: chayote squash, tortillas, oranges and avocados, honey, dried and fresh chiles, chickens and turkeys, eggs, medicinal herbs and copal incense. The road seemed a modern intrusion into a smoky pre-industrial reality.

The road climbed until we came out of the canyons at the first small city, Huehuetenango, where we stopped at a roadside restaurant on the edge of town. Though the place was empty and seemed closed, Victor knew the owner. He called, looked in the kitchen, and came out in a few minutes with his friend Don Pedro. The old man brought us Gallo beers, lemonades and mineral water and said he could make us a limited menu, including a pepian verde that Victor recommended.

Like wolves, we devoured the green mole over local chicken and black beans, with tortillas and avocado slices. After the canyons' sensory overload, the flavors hit me like a bomb. Don Pedro told us the chief ingredients were tomatillos, pumpkin seeds and chiles.

Pepian is a traditional mole of Mexico and Guatemala, though considered a Guatemalan national dish, where it takes many forms, from a soup or caldo to a rich porridge of pumpkin seeds and chiles. For the next two weeks I ate pepians that were soupy, but most were red-chile-and-chicken stews spiced with cinnamon and dried chiles, delicious but never quite as profound as the green one in Huehuetenango. Months later back in Rainbow Lake, I found a correct-sounding recipe in a book of traditional Mayan cooking from the library and made a pepian verde with canned tomatillos. It tasted good but didn't do my memory justice.

In the North, we usually limit the use of tomatillos to green salsa. The fruit does look like a small green tomato, and in fact *tomatillo* is an indigenous

Haying at Asgaard Farm, Au Sable Forks. Nancie Battaglia

berry of the genus *Solanaceae*, related to belladonna, jimsonweed and tomatoes. The stalks grow to six feet high and bear numerous white flowers on a single stem. The calyx hardens to enclose a waxy green or greenish purple berry the size of a golf ball.

The following year, my wife, Sue, and I bought tomatillo seedlings from the Hot House nursery in Saranac Lake and planted them in our raised bed at Rainbow Lake, expecting nothing in our northern conditions. By the middle of August, to our surprise, we had bags of tomatillos. They not only grew like weeds in the Adirondacks, they kept well in the refrigerator and came up by themselves year after year. And they produced the same dark sweet flavor I remembered. I eventually struck on a recipe that at least approximated my memory of the Huehuetenango crossroads. It can be made entirely from organic produce grown in northern New York, Vermont and southern Ontario and Quebec.

Now that we're in the Champlain Valley I make it about once a week from mid-August until late October, always with tortillas and black beans and often with guacamole and fresh sweet corn in season. It keeps well, gets better in the refrigerator, and you can make enchiladas from the leftovers. It also works well with shrimp and pork. You can make a big batch and freeze it, or puree the tomatillos and freeze them in recipe-sized containers.

It's useless to try to recapture the past—like a great jazz solo, a revelatory meal in a deserted restaurant in a charged landscape can only happen once. But if you find a dish that in its flavors and ingredients embodies the meaning and essence of that place—like strawberries and maple syrup, for instance, or fresh brook trout and eggs—it can be useful for understanding and maintaining your connection to the secret harmonies of geography back in the North Country.

Pepian Verde de Rainbow Lake

³/₄ cup dried pumpkin seeds

3 large jalapeño chiles (or Serrano chiles)

4 to 5 large cloves of garlic

1 ¹/₂ lbs. chicken, cut into serving-sized pieces

4 tbsp. olive oil

1 large onion, sliced

1 ¹/₂ lbs. tomatillos, shucked

1 cup chicken broth

Large bunch of cilantro, chopped

Salt, to taste

Throw dried pumpkin seeds into an iron frying pan and brown them until golden (don't scorch), then put them in the food processor, puree and leave them there.

In the dry pan roast the jalapeño and garlic cloves until the chiles are charred and the garlic golden. Set aside. Sauté chicken in olive oil at medium-high heat for 4 minutes a side or until browned. Take pieces out when ready and put in a dish on the side. Sauté the garlic, onion and the seeded chiles together in the pan until soft. Add the shucked tomatillos and stir together for 5 minutes or until soft. Add a cup of chicken broth with the cilantro. Let it simmer for a few minutes to make it soupy. Salt to taste. Transfer the contents of the skillet to the food processor and puree with the pumpkin seeds. It might take two loads. Return the pureed green (or greenish) mole to a 5-quart pan or iron kettle and add more chicken broth until it has the consistency of melted ice cream. You may add the chicken and pan juices at this point, but don't let the meat get dried out. It should simmer for no longer than 30 minutes for bone-in, and about 20 minutes for boneless.

Serves 4 to 5.

Cleaning Up My Karma, *Dale Hobson, Potsdam*

I have frequent wildlife encounters in my kitchen. For years I have bought conventional mousetraps (of which there are none better) and had the unpleasant duty of adding tiny forlorn corpses to the household trash. This fall, during the first cold snap (known, no doubt, as the beginning of the "season" to the frequenters of my rodent

Left: *More wildlife-must-eat photography. This pumpkin did not make it to Halloween.* Bruce Landon, Paul Smiths. Right: *Dessert tonight? Chocolate mous(s)e, perhaps?* Judy Andrus Toporcer, Pierrepont. Below: *Fall harvester and harvested in the Adirondacks.* Nancie Battaglia

resort), I invested in a live trap, hoping to shorten my sentence in hell. Now my morning chore takes me out into the fresh air and down the trail between the deer droppings in the back pasture to perform an act of liberation. There is just this niggling suspicion—that each morning I am releasing the same mouse, who regards a long walk and a warm night in stir as a fair trade for sharp cheddar.

Slow Food: St. Lawrence University Adirondack-Semester Style, *Mary Hussman, Canton*

Every Wednesday morning, from late August until the week before Thanksgiving, I fill the back of my Subaru with waxy recycled produce boxes, but not before I've had a peek inside. I see dozens of fresh eggs and sometimes chickens from Ann and Brian Bennett's Bittersweet Farm, in Heuvelton. Also in Heuvelton, the Kent Family

Growers supply all the produce: in early fall, bags of sweet corn, summer squash and zucchini; a box elbow-deep in lettuce, spinach and greens; another brimful of tomatoes. More boxes stuffed with baby eggplants,

St. Lawrence University Adirondack semester students in their yurt village, in Franklin County. Nancie Battaglia

peppers, basil and melons. Later, the winter squashes come on: Delicata, acorn, many I can't name, as well as broccoli, cauliflower, cabbages, onions, beans, chocolate peppers and sometimes potatoes.

I drive down Route 3, turn in at the Massawepie Boy Scout camp in Childwold, unlock a gate, haul the boxes to a rickety dock and wait for a couple of students to bring the barge across the bay so we can haul the vegetables and eggs over to the yurt village that's home for the semester to 12 St. Lawrence University students. "Mary's here with the vegetables!" they yell, eagerly peering into the boxes before they start stacking the week's array into the mouse-proof bin.

Here, at the remote village they call Arcadia, the students live simply in the woods, away from computers, cell phones and stereos. They take academic courses and field trips that explore their relationship to nature and place through the lens of the Adirondack mountains, lakes and small towns surrounding them. They learn that living simply and sustainably means a lot of hard work: maintaining the small solar array that powers the lights; raking the composting toilet; splitting wood for the stoves and the sauna; hauling, purifying and heating water from the lake for cooking and drinking. And after a day of this, they're ready for a hot and hearty meal.

Every night, two students prepare dinner for the rest of the group and the faculty members who live with them. This past semester, 10 of the 12 students were vegetarian, and so the bounty from the Kents and Bennetts, along with some staples like beans, rice, pasta and bread, formed the basis for three-months' worth of meals. Following are recipes compiled by each cook team.

We loved these student recipes because, whether you're roughing it in the Adirondacks or cooking in the comfort of your own kitchen, all of us have nights when we scrounge from the fridge and pantry to put together a meal after a hard day's work. Mostly, though, we loved how these students remembered to have fun while they cooked. —ER

Bittersweet Farm Chicken, *Peter Tucker and Laura Sisco, Arcadia village*

Under the careful eye of Brian Bennett, kill, pluck, clean and refrigerate a chicken. Gather fresh vegetables from the Kent Family Growers: new potatoes, broccoli, carrots, red peppers, onions and basil. After mourning your chicken for a couple of days, take it out of the fridge and place in a foil-lined 13-by-9-inch pan.

Put on some music and get into your favorite dance pants. Chop the vegetables into robust chunks. Guard your chicken with a colorful fence of chopped veggies. Give the chicken and veggies a luxurious olive oil bath, mixing well to disallow olive oil hoarding.

Mix salt, pepper and chives from your herb garden in a bowl and distribute evenly over chicken and vegetables. Roast chicken and vegetables in a preheated 350° oven. Pull the veggies out after 30 to 40 minutes and keep warm.

Right: St. Lawrence University Adirondack semester students dine alfresco, in Childwold. Nancie Battaglia

Pour a glass of your favorite beverage, grab a book, sit next to the woodstove, and enjoy the aroma of roasting chicken until it's done.

Eggplant for the Phobic, *Raurri Jennings and Erin Hanafin, Arcadia village*

The eggplants are about to turn. Delivered last Wednesday, they've been benchwarmers all week, avoided like the plague. What is it about eggplant that's so daunting? It's not any harder to skin or chop than any other vegetable. There's nothing to be afraid of. Say it again, there's nothing to be afraid of. Don't let the eggplant bully you into a mediocre meal.

Take 4 of those cute little suckers out of the vegetable bin and skin and cube them. In the act of skinning them they become less intimidating, like speaking in front of an audience while pretending everyone is naked. Next, throw the cubes into a pot of boiling salted water until they are slightly squishy. While you are boiling away your phobia, chop up 4 cloves of garlic and throw them into a bowl of olive oil, $^1/_2$ cup, give or take, because psychology isn't an exact science.

St. Lawrence University students share meal duties in the kitchen yurt during their Adirondack semester, Childwold.
Nancie Battaglia

Next, drain the eggplant, dump it into the bowl of oil and garlic, and mash it up while thinking of your worst childhood memory. Put out some grated cheese, some tortillas and raisins. Plop a spoonful or two of eggplant in the middle of a tortilla and top with the cheese and raisins. Roll it up and put it on a greased baking sheet. Repeat until the eggplant is gone, then bake at 350° for 20 minutes. When you pull them out of the oven, admire your cathartic little burritos and serve them to your 12 closest friends. They'll be proud of your courage in conquering your fear of eggplant.

St. Lawrence University student Laura Sisco in the Adirondack semester program kitchen yurt, in Childwold. Nancie Battaglia

Baked Delicata Squash with Maple Syrup,
Katie Powers and Zena Wolcott-MacCausland,
Arcadia village

They got shoved into the back of the screened-in, mouse-proof vegetable cabinet, behind the more recognizable peppers, onions and tomatoes. There were seven of them, oblong with stark green stripes across their smooth skin. The normal fare at Arcadia typically features more common vegetables, and the eggplant, root vegetables or unfamiliar varieties of squash tend to be overlooked by the amateur chef. But these unique Delicata represent the rich, abundant harvest offered by the soils of the North Country. As summer fades into the colder nights of fall, the beds of thick, spiny green plants produce an array of hardy vegetables of every shape and size. Tonight is cool and crisp. Zena and I survey the veggie cabinet, spot the seven colorful squash, and decide to bake them. Using a method she remembers from home, Zena creates a tray full of sweet, warm nourishment that helps us welcome the new season.

Heat oven to 375°. Cut squash in half lengthwise, and scoop the seeds into the compost bucket. Place cut side down on a baking sheet, add a bit of water and bake for about 30 minutes or until soft. Remove them from the oven, turn them over and add a couple slivers of butter and a couple of tbsp. of North Country maple syrup. Bake for another 10 minutes or until syrup has slightly caramelized. Serve and enjoy.

Chilly Evening Chili, *Kate McCarthy and Dominique Edgerly, Arcadia village*

By Monday night the vegetable cabinet is looking sparse since the last shipment of vegetables was almost a week ago. There's a chill tonight as autumn sets in, the perfect weather for wool sweaters and the best kind of homemade, heartwarming meal: chili. The measurements are up to you, depending on the company. Is it a big family gathering or just the two of you? Either way, just plop these ingredients in a big pot and, as they simmer, sit down for a hot cup of tea and a nice chat with a friend.

Tomato paste (add water)
Fresh cut tomatoes
Beans (black, kidney, garbanzo or whatever's on hand)
Peppers
Onions
Salt and black pepper
Your favorite salsa
Pineapple (for a little bit of pizzazz!)

Bottom of the Barrel Chili, *Nathan Basch and Emily Rooney, Arcadia village*

Cooking dinner on Tuesday nights is always a daunting task since the vegetables don't come till Wednesdays. In the fridge we have butter, soy milk, corn and leftover cabbage salad. The vegetable bin is not much better. There we have garlic, onions, two squishy squashes and some overripe tomatoes. In our storage room at the Boy Scout lodge across the lake, we have several cans of beans and other assorted vegetables as well as frozen tomato sauce. Chili, we decide, is a delicious way to use up what few remaining vegetables we have. After a quick kayak across the lake to grab supplies, we're ready. Just mix everything together and heat.

Tomato sauce
Tomato paste
Leftover corn
Random beans
Mushy tomatoes
Last remnants of yellow squash
Onions
Garlic
Chili powder and whatever other spices we find

St. Lawrence University Adirondack semester students dine alfresco, in Childwold. Nancie Battaglia

Morewood, *Stevie and Jim Michaelson, Canton*

My uncle, Tom Farley, a lifelong resident of southern St. Lawrence County, introduced us to a drink recipe he acquired long ago at Camp Morewood, a Canadian hunting camp. His daughter, Judy Constantine, now of Florida, provided details she remembered from her childhood.

The drink combines maple syrup, blended Canadian whiskey and warm water in a straight-sided short water glass. It is imbibed by hunters before a hearty breakfast of eggs, pancakes and sausages, followed by a long day in the cold Canadian woods.

Specifically: A teaspoon is set in the glass and maple syrup poured to the top of the "bowl" part of the spoon. Equal parts of whiskey and warm water are added, then stirred to blend.

We have not heard of a Morewood outside of the North Country, especially when used as a breakfast aperitif.

Venison Chops in Red Wine Sauce, *George Arnold, Potsdam*

Although I have eaten as a vegetarian for the past 20-odd years, you can't really be a chef in the North Country and not know at least one recipe for venison.

4 venison chops,
cut at least 1 inch thick

³/₈ cup red wine vinegar

1 oz. olive oil

1 shallot, minced

¹/₄ bay leaf

1 sprig of fresh thyme

¹/₂ tsp. grated orange peel

1 tbsp. red currant jelly

1 tsp. orange juice

Salt and pepper

Mix together the vinegar, oil, shallot, herbs and orange peel. Marinate the chops in this for at least 2 hours. Remove the chops and save the marinade. Dry the chops and cook them in a frying pan, about 4 minutes per side until done to your liking. Remove the chops to the serving platter and add the marinade, jelly and juice to the hot pan. Let it simmer until sauce consistency. Remove the thyme and bay leaf and add salt and pepper, to taste.

The Bluff Gang of 1990: Rodney "Mr. Clean" Clarke, Bill "Pilgrim" MacMillan, Pete Kaminski, Bill Brown. Back row: Gibb Newton, Roger Sullivan, Don Brownell, Dave Corse, Chris Hamilton. Submitted by Bill MacMillan, of Island Park, who wrote: "My first experience with North Country hunting changed my life. These men had a permanent and profound effect on me. True woodsmen and sportsmen." Photographer unknown

Venison Roast Dinner, *Edna and Susan Mosher via Carol Pearsall, Johnsburg*

*W*hen my children were in kindergarten the teachers and mothers arranged a Thanksgiving dinner with venison and bear for the children. Wanting to follow the seasons, I phoned Edna Mosher, who is a very good cook, and spoke with her daughter Susan, who follows in her mother's footsteps when it comes to cooking. I asked if she and her mother would share a recipe for wild game. A couple of days later the following recipes arrived for venison roast, mashed potatoes, gravy, steamed green beans and buttermilk biscuits.

Venison roast:
Place a 4-lb. venison roast in a pan with about 1 cup of water; sprinkle with salt and pepper. Cover the meat tightly with foil; place in 350° oven for about 1 hour and 45 minutes.

Take meat out of dish, cover and let set while preparing the gravy. To serve, carve meat as thin as possible.

Gravy:
Bring the juices from the roasting pan (minus the fat) to a boil in a saucepan. Place a rounded tbsp. of flour with a $^1/_4$ cup of water in a jar and shake until well blended. Slowly pour the flour-water mix, a little at a time, into the boiling pan juices, stirring constantly with a wire whip, until the gravy is the thickness you like.

Mashed potatoes:
Peel and wash potatoes, put into a pot with water to cover, add 1 tsp. salt. Boil potatoes until tender. Drain off the water; mash with a potato masher or beat with a mixer until fluffy with a little milk and 2 tbsp. of butter.

Steamed green beans:
Snap the ends off the green beans, wash, put in kettle with a little water; steam until tender, about 20 to 25 minutes.

Buttermilk biscuits:
2 cups flour
2 tsp. baking powder
$^1/_3$ cup Crisco
$^1/_2$ tsp. salt

Cut mixture together. Add enough buttermilk to moisten dough so you can roll it. Roll the dough out on a floured board, cut with a round cutter (you can use a glass). Place on a baking sheet. Bake in a 350° oven until lightly brown, about 25 to 35 minutes.

My husband, who is always on the alert to make me a better cook, recently brought me a lovely biscuit cutter and explained to me that he was told you do not turn the cutter as you cut the biscuits as that will seal the edges and keep them from raising properly in the oven. You push down on the cutter and pick straight up.

One-Pan Adirondack Camp Dinner, *Phil Greenland, Brighton*

A *pair of arts folks fell in love with the Adirondacks. Being terribly impulsive (as arts folks are), we ended up with a real fixer-upper and quickly discovered we had to find meals we could make without the benefit of a working kitchen. This is a favorite.*

4 pork chops

2 tbsp. vegetable oil

2 tbsp. flour

1/3 cup grated Parmesan cheese

Healthy dash of salt

Pepper, to taste

4 potatoes, thinly sliced

2 small onions, thinly sliced

3 cubes beef bouillon

3/4 cup hot water

Dash of lemon juice

Heat the oil in a large skillet. Coat the pork chops with flour and put in the skillet. Brown about 4 minutes on each side.

In a bowl, mix the Parmesan, salt and pepper. Sprinkle half the Parmesan cheese mixture over the pork chops. Layer chops with the potatoes. Sprinkle with remaining Parmesan mixture. Top it with the onion slices. In another bowl, combine the beef bouillon cubes and hot water. Add a dash of lemon juice and pour over the layered pork chops. Cover the pan and reduce heat to low. Simmer 45 minutes, until vegetables are soft. Pork chops should have an internal temperature of 160° when done.

Serves 4.

Lumber Camp Breakfast, *Lesley Mace Knoll, Long Lake*

My mother was Ora Haché Mace. Her mother, Anna Loport Haché, was a cook in a lumber camp outside Tupper Lake from about 1910 to 1920. My mother said Grandmother made a lumberjack breakfast by cooking a lot of bacon in a skillet. Then, the bacon fat was

used to fry bread slices with a hole cut in the middle (she used a glass or muffin cutter). An egg was cracked into the hole, cooked, and the whole thing flipped and fried until done. These were served with the bacon, plus steak, potatoes and lots of coffee. It was what was needed by lumberjacks to fuel their hard work until suppertime.

Roscoe, Basyl ("Tuck"), Elva and "Shine," circa 1950, at the family camp in Parishville, on the West Branch of the St. Regis River. The stone barbecue pit is still there, albeit more lopsided and patched.
Photographer unknown

Sweet and Spicy Fall Soup, *Yvona Fast, Lake Clear*

4 cups chicken or vegetable broth

1 small butternut squash, peeled, seeded and cut up

2 sweet potatoes

1 turnip

2 white potatoes

1 or 2 carrots

1 tbsp. olive oil

2 large onions

2 stalks celery

2 cups kale, finely chopped

3 cloves garlic

1 tsp. chili powder

1 lb. silken tofu

2 tart apples

Juice of half a lime (about 2 to 3 tbsp.)

1 cup walnuts, minced

1/2 cup snipped chives

Bring 1 qt. of broth to a boil. Add the butternut squash, and cook. While squash is cooking, peel and dice sweet potatoes; add. Then peel and dice the turnip, and add; then the white potatoes and carrots. The order is important, because the vegetables vary in cooking times.

While vegetables are cooking, heat the oil in a medium-sized skillet. Peel and dice the onion, and add; wash and slice the celery and chop the kale, and stir in; peel and mince the garlic fine, and add, along with the chili powder. Cook, stirring occasionally, over low heat, 15 to 20 minutes until the vegetables are tender. Be careful not to burn.

Remove vegetables from heat. With a slotted spoon, remove them to a food processor. Puree, in batches if necessary, along with 1 lb. silken tofu. When done, stir back into the broth, combining until uniform. Then stir in the sautéed vegetables in the skillet (onion, kale, celery and garlic). Peel, core and shred the apple; combine with lime juice. Remove soup from heat and stir in the apple along with the lime juice. Adjust for seasonings; you may wish to add a bit more salt, chili or lime. Serve hot, garnished with chopped nuts and snipped chives.

Serves 16.

Jars of color and plenty in Rob and Winny Sachno's Potsdam root cellar. Paula Schechter, Potsdam

Canning

I haven't used my pressure canner in years, but I think it's coming out of mothballs—essential for storing low-acid foods. Mostly, I've been canning high-acid foods using a water-bath canner. I love canning tomatoes. Once you've got the simple technique down, it's a high-yield effort that takes care of all the excess fruit you've nurtured from seed or seedling. Ditto for applesauce. And, if you watch local markets, it's well worth it to buy large quantities of New York State peaches and pears when they come into season. I make the effort because it's a realistic way to extend my source of locally grown foods into the winter, because it's good to eat food preserved without preservatives, and, maybe mostly, because the jars look so beautiful on the pantry shelves. —ER

Putting By, *Winny Sachno, Potsdam*

Here's a list of stored up "goods." I don't do all of these things every year (beef lasts several years; I do chicken every other year). I do what veggies and fruits come my way and plant next year according to what's left by spring.

Stored fresh:

Apples: Cortland

Cabbage: red and green

Carrots

Cider vinegar

Corn: dried for cornmeal

Garlic

Maple syrup

Onions

Potatoes: Yukon Gold, Kennebec, Pontiac

Rutabagas

Sauerkraut

Squash: Delicata, butternut, pie pumpkins

Sweet potatoes

Canned:

Applesauce, apple butter

Beef

Blueberries

Boar, wild

Cherries

Chicken

Cider: apple, pear

Goat

Jams: blueberry, blackberry, currant, raspberry, strawberry, wild grape, rose hip

Juices: elderberry, rhubarb, black currant, wild grape

Lamb

Soup stock: chicken and beef

Strawberries

Venison

Kramer Kosher Dills, *David Sommerstein, Pierrepont*

According to my grandmother, Frances Kramer, my grandfather's father fled Kreminitz, Russia, around the turn of the last century to avoid mandatory military conscription. He traveled across western Europe by doing work as a tailor. He carried with him the Kramer family pickle recipe. It's distinguished by the fact that it uses no vinegar, only water and lots of strong spices and peppers. A jar of these pickles formed the centerpiece on tables at our wedding party in 2003. The guests toasted with pickles.

Per wide-mouthed jar:

6 to 10 fresh, slender, crisp pickling cucumbers, with no blemishes on skin

1 heaping tbsp. kosher salt

2 to 3 cloves fresh garlic

1 stem and head fresh dill

1 tbsp. pickling spices

2 to 6 cayenne peppers (those longish, thin, deep red ones), depending how spicy you want

Sterilize jars and lids in boiling hot water (or in dish washer). Clean cucumbers of dirt lightly, then chill them in a bath of ice water for 1 to 2 hours.

Meanwhile, add the remaining ingredients to each jar.

When the cukes are ready, pack them into the jars without bruising them. Don't pack too many into each jar, or they'll come out mushy. Fill the jars with water. Seal with the lids so there's no leakage. Shake jars well to mix everything together.

Store for 3 to 4 weeks in a cool, dark place before opening to eat.

NCPR reporter David Sommerstein and wife Lisa Lazenby's sukkah, celebrating the Jewish harvest holiday of Sukkot during which meals are enjoyed outside. Oh, and it happens to coincide with the start of the major league baseball playoff season. David Sommerstein, Canton

Green Tomato Pickles, *Elise Widlund, North River*

W*hen I was growing up, my father insisted on a victory garden that could feed the entire town. He loved turning over the soil, getting his hands into the rich dirt and watching the seeds develop into our table sustenance. In his enthusiasm, there were always tomatoes that could not ripen in the allotted sun timetable. What to do with all the green tomatoes? My mother came to this situation armed with the family recipe for green tomato pickles from Grandma Bellinger, who lived from 1839 to 1924.*

Cook tomatoes until tender, but not falling apart, in:

1 part vinegar

4 parts water

A little sugar

Wash and slice 1 peck (¹/₄ bushel) green tomatoes. Layer with sprinkles of salt. Let stand overnight. Rinse and drain.

Syrup:

1 qt. vinegar

8 cups brown sugar

1 tbsp. whole cloves

1 stick cinnamon (1 tsp. ground)

Place cooked tomatoes in crock or jars and cover with syrup. Let stand a couple of weeks.

Claudia's gourmet Adirondack bread-and-butter pickles, Indian Lake. Nancie Battaglia

Sauerkraut, *Ellen Rocco, DeKalb*

I've had good years and bad years with sauerkraut. In truth, the bad years are my fault. Sauerkraut, a simple two-ingredient concoction, does require some tending while it ferments. In years when I've neglected the crock, bad sauerkraut is the result. But if I give it a quick skim occasionally and keep the material covering the mixture clean, the payoff is worth it. Fresh sauerkraut is wonderfully crisp and refreshing. The recipe and process is standard.

5 lbs. very finely sliced/shredded cabbage

3 tbsp. kosher or canning salt

In a large bowl, mix cabbage (be sure to weigh cabbage after shredding, not while the heads are intact) with salt. Let stand for a few minutes. Pack a portion of the cabbage into a crock or large glass jar. Press down until liquid begins to appear. Repeat for remaining cabbage. Fresh cabbage yields much more "juice" than older cabbage. You may have to continue to press down occasionally for the first day or so to draw out sufficient liquid. If liquid still doesn't cover cabbage, add additional salt water (about 1 tsp. of salt to a cup of water). Place a plate or other flat, clean object on top of crock, weight down with a jar of water and cover with a clean cloth. Check every few days as sauerkraut ferments. Skim off top layer of cabbage if it becomes soft or discolored. It won't ruin the rest. Begin tasting for "doneness" after about 10 days to 2 weeks. You can store finished sauerkraut in the refrigerator for many weeks. Canning works well too. Check *Ball Blue Book of Preserving* or Cooperative Extension information booklets for details.

Once you're confident about "krauting," try mixing other crisp, shredded vegetables into the cabbage—turnips, carrots and onions work well. Last year we added bits of hot peppers. This was a hit.

Note from Chef George: When you live in the Northeast you can't think of autumn and not think of apples. John Chapman, born in Massachusetts in 1774, is also known as Johnny Appleseed. Schoolchildren who learn his name hear the tale of how he sowed apple seeds throughout New England. Sweet story, but as author Michael Pollan (*The Botany of Desire*) has noted, these were cider apples rather than eating apples. Since most of these apples were destined to become hard cider, Chapman was in reality spreading the gift of alcohol to the early settlers. Given their hard life, I'm sure it was appreciated.

Granny Smith Apple "Aphrodisiac," *Jonathan Brown, Canton*

I made this once for a woman I was dating in San Francisco. After her first bite, she said, "I can't believe how attracted I am toward you just because you made this."

4 Granny Smith apples, sliced

¼ lb. goat cheese

2 oz. walnut halves

2 tbsp. honey

Place a small pat of goat cheese on each apple slice, then place half a walnut on top of each pat, and drizzle honey over each slice.

Serves 4.

Apple-Ginger-Lime Chutney, *Susan Stuck, Charlotte VT*

Wonderful with sharp cheddar and crackers, or roast pork or chicken, or lamb curry.

3 cups cider vinegar

4 cups sugar

16 apples that keep their shape when cooked, such as Golden Delicious or Granny Smith, peeled, cored and sliced into ½-inch pieces

4 limes, scrubbed, cut into small wedges, wedges sliced into thin pieces

2 garlic cloves, minced

1 tbsp. salt, or more if you like a more pungent flavor

1 to 2 tsp. dried red pepper flakes, Aleppo pepper or ground chile

2 tsp. ground coriander

½ tsp. ground cardamom (optional)

16 oz. dried mangos, sliced

8 to 12 oz. crystallized ginger, thinly sliced

In a big, wide pot, boil cider and sugar for 5 minutes. Add apples, limes, garlic, salt, pepper flakes, coriander and cardamom. Simmer over low heat until apples are soft, about 20 minutes. Add mango and ginger slices and simmer until the chutney is thick, about 20 minutes longer. Ladle the hot chutney into hot sterilized pint jars, leaving ½-inch headspace. Cover with new lids and screwbands. You should hear a "pop" from the jars after a minute or 2, indicating the seal is good. If you don't hear a pop, process the jars for 10 minutes in a boiling water bath.

Makes 5 to 6 pints.

Apple Tree Haiku, *Dale Hobson, Potsdam*

The grape-choked apple
struggles fruitless toward the light—
uproot all the vines.

Applesauce with Cinnamon Candies, *Cheryl Maid, Saranac Lake*

When you are making fresh applesauce, instead of adding cinnamon, use those wonderful small, spicy red cinnamon imperial candies that you find in bags around Valentine's Day. As a young girl, I loved stirring them into the hot apples after my mom put them through the Foley Food Mill.

Applesauce in a Crock-Pot, *Marybeth Peabody, Keene*

One day last winter, my husband was in a rush and decided to try making applesauce in the Crock-Pot. The unexpected results gave a flavor and texture that is truly amazing, warm or cold.

About 15 large apples, Honeycrisp or any fairly tart apple

Peel, core and slice apples and place in Crock-Pot. You can heap them up pretty high because they will cook down quickly. No need to put water in the bottom of the pot. Cook on low for 12 hours. We usually cook it overnight and awake to the wonderful smell. When fully cooked the apples should have a reddish caramel color, but certainly not be burned. You will have to experiment with the time because all Crock-Pots are different. The apples may require squashing with a potato masher to obtain a sauce consistency.

Cran-Apple-Grape Sauce, *Laurie Smith, Canton*

2 cups apples, sliced (not peeled)

2 cups cranberries

1 cup Concord grapes

Sugar (or sweetener of choice), to taste

Wash all the fruit; blend in a food processor or high-powered blender (in batches as necessary). Transfer to a medium pot, cook on medium heat until it boils, then lower heat and simmer. Add some sweetener. Cool. After cooling, sweeten to taste. A bit of lemon or orange goes well in this, too. Proportions of fruit are purely subjective. Caution: Concord grapes can be overpowering.

Serves 20.

Above: *Washing apples at Bradbury's Orchard, Keene.* Photographer unknown.
Left: *A North Country apple.* Nancie Battaglia

Cousin Betty, *Todd Moe, Norwood*

Everyone knows Betty Crocker isn't a real person. And her equally fictitious portrait on cookbooks has accommodated cultural expectations throughout the decades. She's a marketing tool hatched back in the early 1920s.

But I *am* related to the woman who helped create the Betty Crocker image.

Over a Thanksgiving meal with my family a few years ago, the subjects of food and broadcasting came up. Grandpa Moe announced that I wasn't the first radio announcer in the family. Marjorie Husted, his cousin on his mother's side, worked for Washburn-Crosby Company (which later became General Mills) in Minneapolis as field representative for home economics in 1921. The department was eventually renamed the Betty Crocker Homemaking Service, with Husted as director. How the name was created is another story. But the short version goes that "Betty" was chosen as a common woman's name at the time, and "Crocker" came from the late director of the company, William Crocker. So, Marjorie Husted was the woman who replied to requests for household advice and recipes from customers. She signed her letters, "Betty Crocker." In 1924, Washburn-Crosby Company bought a radio station (WCCO), and Husted hosted the "Betty Crocker Cooking School of the Air" on Friday mornings throughout the Midwest.

OK, so technically I'm not related to Betty Crocker. But the woman who was the voice of Betty Crocker on radio shows for years was my first cousin, twice removed. For her listeners, she wielded a mighty spatula—still, I wonder if she had to deal with weather forecasts.

Grandma's Crow's Nest, *Kelly Trombley, Potsdam*

One of my favorite childhood memories is eating my Grandma Pruner's Crow's Nest. When I was very little, I wondered where she got the crows.

4 medium tart apples, sliced

1 cup flour

2 tbsp. baking powder

¹/₄ tsp. salt

1 ¹/₄ tsp. cinnamon

¹/₄ cup sugar

3 tbsp. shortening

¹/₃ cup milk

Place apples in well-greased pan or Pyrex dish. Dot with butter, sprinkle with sugar and cinnamon. Mix flour, baking powder, salt and sugar. Sift twice. Cut in the shortening with a blender. Add milk to make a soft dough and spread over apples. (Wet back of spoon to promote better spreading of dough.) Bake at 400° for 25 to 30 minutes. Make sure apples are cooked well. When cooked completely, invert on plate. Serve hot or cold with ice cream.

Serves 6.

Getting ready to make a North Country apple pie. Nancie Battaglia

Fruit Crisp for Fall, *Yvona Fast, Lake Clear*

*B*lueberries that we picked in the summer and stored in the freezer make a nice addition to this dish.

4 apples

2 tbsp. lemon juice, divided

1 tsp. all-purpose flour

¹/₄ cup brown sugar

1 pear

1 cup sour cherries

³/₄ cup blueberries

²/₃ cup walnuts

Topping:

6 tbsp. butter

¹/₄ cup brown sugar

¹/₄ cup all-purpose flour

¹/₄ cup whole-wheat flour

¹/₃ cup ground walnuts

1 tsp. cinnamon

¹/₂ tsp. salt

1 cup oats

Preheat oven to 375°. Butter a 9-by-9-inch baking dish.

Peel, core and slice apples. Spread a layer on bottom of dish. Sprinkle with 1 tbsp. of the lemon juice. Top with cherries and sprinkle with flour and brown sugar. Peel, core and slice the pear. Layer on top of the apples; sprinkle with remaining tbsp. of lemon juice. Sprinkle the berries (blueberries work well) and walnuts over all. Melt the butter in a medium saucepan. Add the brown sugar and stir to combine. Add the flours, ground nuts, cinnamon and salt. Stir in the oats, and mix well.

Spread the topping evenly over the fruit. Bake 45 to 50 minutes. If the top browns too quickly, lower the heat a bit and cover with aluminum foil.

Serves 6.

North Country apples at a produce stand, Malone. Nancie Battaglia

Honey Cake for the New Year, *Jackie Sauter, Canton*

The Jewish New Year (Rosh Hashanah) is celebrated in the early fall. It's traditional to taste honey to welcome a sweet and happy new year and this traditional recipe has been in my family for generations. My beloved copy, hand-written for me long ago by my mother, is covered with the spots and stains of years of holiday cake-making. Honey is hygroscopic, which means that it can draw moisture from the air and so cakes made with honey tend to stay moist and flavorful. This one's a keeper.

1 cup sugar

1 cup honey

2 eggs

1 tsp. vanilla

1 cup strong cold black coffee

3 cups flour

1 tsp. allspice

1 tsp. baking soda

1 tsp. baking powder

³/₄ cup vegetable oil

1 cup raisins

1 cup chopped walnuts

Preheat oven to 350°.

Mix sugar and honey, add eggs, vanilla and coffee. Blend well.

Sift dry ingredients together; add to liquid batter. Mix thoroughly, then add oil slowly. Mix thoroughly until ingredients are completely blended. Pour batter into greased and floured tube pan or rectangular pan. Sprinkle with raisins and nuts and pat them down just a bit.

Bake about an hour, just until a tester comes out clean.

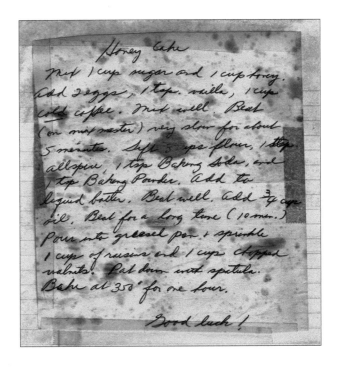

Following the Nose, *Dale Hobson, Potsdam*

I t will be a small Thanksgiving this year, just the three of us, and a few friends

later for dessert. No long drive, no folding children's table tacked on the end of a

fully extended oak antique. No bevy of aunts acting as sous-chefs to the baster-

wielding matriarch. But it is only a short quiet pause, after grandparents and parents

have left us only memory and a few bits of

good china, and before we ourselves occupy

the head of a three-generation table. Terry has

all the makings of a pretty fierce matriarch her-

self. So we give thanks for our lives and for the

lives that came before, and the lives that will

come after, following their noses to partake in

the feast.

Above: *Mike and Meagan Erickson enjoy the Thanksgiving meal while Gabby, Gracie and Charlie can only hope.* Cheryl Erickson, Brant Lake. Below: *Breakfast at Johns Brook Lodge, Keene Valley.* Nancie Battaglia

Jackie's Mom's Pumpkin Cake, *Jackie Sauter, Canton*

*T*here's Honey Cake for the Jewish New Year and this cake for the rest of the season. My mom has been baking this beloved cake forever. So have my aunts, my cousins and all the other women in my family—me too! This is the perfect cake for every occasion. It's easy, delicious, addictive.

4 eggs

2 cups sugar

1 ¹/₂ cups Wesson oil

2 cups canned pumpkin (unseasoned, or use drained fresh-cooked)

2 cups flour

2 tsp. baking powder

2 tsp. baking soda

¹/₂ tsp. salt

3 tsp. cinnamon

8 oz. of chocolate chips (or about a cup of chopped chocolate)

Cream eggs and sugar. Add remaining ingredients. Mix well. Pour into greased Bundt or tube pan. Bake at 350° for 60 or so minutes, until a tester just comes out clean. Cool a bit, then remove from pan while cake is still a little warm. Cover cake loosely with plastic wrap while still warm to preserve moisture.

Pumpkins at Rulf's, Peru. Nancie Battaglia

Pumpkin Bread, *Jan DeWaters, Potsdam*

*O*ne time my college roommate and I mixed up a batch of pumpkin bread before travel-ing the one-and-a-half hours from New Hampshire to my parents' house in Maine. We kneaded the dough and then nestled it into a large bowl, covered with a clean towel in the backseat of the car. We set off on our trip and, of course, promptly forgot all about the rising dough. When we arrived at my parents' house and unpacked the car, we found the dough had escaped the bowl, onto the car seat. We salvaged most of the dough, got it into pans to rise and bake—and it was the most delicious pumpkin bread ever.

2 tbsp. yeast

¹/₄ cup lukewarm water

A pinch of salt

¹/₄ cup sugar

1 ³/₄ cups milk, scalded

1 tsp. salt

2 ¹/₂ cups flour, mixed until smooth

2 cups pureed, cooked pumpkin

¹/₄ cup melted shortening, mixed well

Combine yeast, lukewarm water and a pinch of salt; let stand to soften yeast.

Mix sugar, milk and salt in a separate bowl. Stir, cool to lukewarm, then add to softened yeast. Mix flour, cooked pumpkin and shortening; add to bowl. Stir in enough flour to make a soft dough (about 5 ¹/₂ to 6 additional cups; up to half the flour may be whole-wheat). Turn dough onto floured board, cover and let rest 10 minutes. Knead until elastic and smooth. Cover, let rise until double. Punch down dough, knead a bit and divide into three. Place into prepared bread pans, let rise about 30 minutes. Bake at 400° for 15 minutes; reduce heat to 375° for another 20 to 30 minutes.

Makes 3 loaves.

Cranberry Chocolate Chip Cookies, *Evelyn Greene, North Creek*

³/₄ cup shortening

1 cup light brown sugar

2 large eggs

1 tsp. vanilla

2 ¹/₄ cups flour

¹/₄ tsp. baking soda

1 cup cranberries

1 cup chopped walnuts

1 cup chocolate chips

Cream first 4 ingredients. Add next 2, stir well. Stir in remaining 3 ingredients. Refrigerate for 1 hour. Preheat oven to 350°. Drop dough by heaping tbsp. on a greased cookie pan, bake about 20 minutes.

Note: You can use dried sweetened cranberries, but I like small, whole, fresh cranberries picked from an Adirondack bog, or halved regular-sized ones. The small ones are a wonderful contrast with the sweetness of the chocolate when they pop in your mouth. I call them "sour bombs."

The House of History, *Anne Werley Smallman, Malone*

The *Malone Cookbook* was first published in 1882 by the Women's Aid Society of the First Congregational Church of Malone, as a means to raise funds for the construction of the third (and current) church building. (Former U.S. Vice-President and Malone resident William A. Wheeler was chair of the building committee and contributed his own funds generously to the project. This building, built 1883–1884, is on the National Register of Historic Places.) Recipes from the community were solicited and the cookbook was popular enough that expanded editions were subsequently published in 1888, 1898, 1903, 1908, 1917, 1923, 1968 and 1982. The fifth edition was abridged and published in New York Type for the Blind. In early editions, local businesses purchased ads; many of these ads are reproduced in the Centennial (ninth) Edition.

The Museum Day School Program of the Franklin County Historical and Museum Society hosts fourth graders from each elementary school in Franklin County. Each class visits the House of History for a tour of the museum, hands-on craft demonstrations, and milk and molasses cookies. Until recently, the cookies were baked in the wood-fired cookstove in the kitchen of the museum. Many volunteers associate the recipe with Mrs. Helen Cosgrove, although its exact provenance is not certain. The Museum Day School Program is more than 30 years old, and continues to give fourth graders from throughout the county a hands-on experience (and taste) of local history.

House of History Molasses Cookies, *Mary Ann Tallon, submission for the* Malone Cookbook

4 cups flour

1 cup sugar

1 tsp. salt

1 tsp. baking soda

1 tsp. ginger

2 tsp. cinnamon

2 eggs

1 cup molasses

1 cup shortening

Sift together first 4 ingredients. Blend together the rest of the ingredients, mixing well. Roll walnut-sized chunks of dough in a bowl of sugar, then place on greased cookie sheet. Bake at 350° for 10 minutes.

Three Bowls, *Dale Hobson, Potsdam*

There has been much talk lately about the so-called "hundred-mile diet"—living primarily or completely on foods grown and prepared within 100 miles of where you live. Economy looks very different when one of the factors in the bottom line is, "Do I know who grew this? Do I know who made this?"

Lately, my wife and I have been getting a lot of use out of three bowls, survivors of a set of four thrown and fired more than 30 years ago in the house where we lived with our potter friend, Annie. Any vessel would do to keep the soup from our lap, but the feel and the history and the look of these particular bowls add to the savor of anything contained within. The profile is a simple unbroken curve of high-fired stoneware with a milk-white crackled glaze. Each is decorated with a few seemingly offhand brushstrokes that suggest a cobalt flower with translucent leaves. And each has an elegant bulb handle, itself a tiny separately-thrown pot, half closed at the top, with its foot smoothly mated to the curve of the body. The notch is a perfect fit for the thumb web when the bowl is cradled in the palm to feel the warmth within. They are not identical as machine-ware, but are meticulously consistent, in the way a quality crafter demonstrates focus and integrity.

They were made as gifts for my mother-in-law, and returned to our hutch after her death a few years back. So whenever I use one now, I think of Annie, and I remember my mother-in-law,

Above: *Three bowls and autumn harvest.* Right: *Onions drying, Rivermede Farm, Keene Valley.* Nancie Battaglia (2)

Betty, as I turn it slowly in my hand to admire. What would we own and what would we pass over, if this was the standard toward which our desires aspired?

GardenShare's Local Harvest Potluck Dinner, *November 2006, Potsdam*

Apples

Apple crisp

Apple pie

Baked beans with onions and maple syrup

Baked rutabaga

Beef stew

Beet salad

Blackberry pudding cake

Blueberry muffins

Bok choy, broccoli, carrots and garlic stir-fry

Cabbage salad

Chicken and vegetable stew

Chocolate-mint pudding cake

Cornbread

Cottage cheese

Goat cheese

Green pepper casserole

Green salad

Honey-glazed chickpeas

Hot Italian bison sausage with tomato sauce

Jacob's cattle beans

Leg of lamb

Mashed potatoes

Oven-fried chicken

Parsnips

Pea soup

Pumpkin loaf

Roasted tomato and pasta casserole

Roasted vegetables

Rosemary focaccia

Salmon cakes

Salsa

Sauerkraut and kielbasa casserole

Spicy potatoes

Spinach salad

Steamed kale

Three sisters stew

Venison stew

Winter squash with maple syrup

Winter

First you stoke the stove, then you stoke the belly. Where once a little toast or a bowl of cereal would do to start the day, now a stack of hotcakes is wanted, aswim with butter and syrup, or bug-eyed eggs with sizzling sausage and home fries.

After shoveling the walk and the driveway and the roof, you want to know where the stew is. You want the second helping of pasta, a big baked potato with sour cream and chives, a garlicky slab of roast pork. Now you would indeed like fries with that, and gravy on the fries, too. The days are too short, and the season is too long.

The holidays come like candy to a sick child—morale food—cakes and cookies, pies and pastries, fruitcake and fudge—but the deep freeze goes on month by month, after the sugar rush ends. Stir-crazy, you may find yourself clumping along for miles on snowshoes, with no better reward at the end than hot cocoa with cinnamon and a twist of fried dough. Or you may just skip the snowshoes and sit by the window, warming your hands on the steaming mug, to wait out the laggard thaw. **—Dale Hobson**

Left: *Young ice fisherman, Lake Colby.* Nancie Battaglia

Winter Toughs, *Ellen Rocco, DeKalb*

In northern New York and Vermont, and across Canada, winter separates the amateur—visitor or tourist—from those of us who are, at least in our own minds, the truly tough. We enjoy scaring new neighbors with tales of winters past—30° or 40° below zero for nights on end, snow piled to the top of first-floor windows. This somewhat perverse climate boasting may be in decline with the onset of global warming, but odds are it will remain cold enough to warrant the decidedly robust recipes North Country Public Radio listeners contributed to this section.

Backcountry skiers share an alfresco lunch in the St. Regis Wilderness Area. Nancie Battaglia

It seems particularly apt to start the winter offerings with a story and two terrific comfort-food suggestions from the station's membership director, June Peoples, whose Southern accent and skills as a hostess may fool you into believing she could never be tough enough to survive our climate. She's lasted more than a decade and, we suspect, does her own climate boasting when she talks to her family below the Mason-Dixon.

October 1998—The Brochure Looks Nice

You want to move where? Canton, New York. Hmm, never heard of it. Where is that exactly? Northern New York? Mountains, gorgeous fall colors, great people, fabulous public radio station, vibrant arts community—sounds wonderful. When do we leave?

Stage One—Denial

It's November, it's been below freezing and the snow hasn't stopped since October; there is more snow on the ground than I have seen (cumulatively) in my entire life. This must be a fluke. No? *Seriously?* I don't believe it. I'm sure it'll warm up soon.

Comfort food therapy: Enjoy a bowl of warm bean and sage soup with herb and cheese cornbread. Check frequently to see if the weather is clearing up.

Stage Two—Anger

December (still snowing): I'm sorry—the average temperature is below freezing for *how* many months of the year?

January: It's -30°? **What? N-e-g-a-t-i-v-e t-h-i-r-t-y d-e-g-r-e-e-s!!!???** It's like this every year? Oh … my … God … I cannot believe you didn't share this interesting tidbit of information before now.

Comfort food therapy: Piping hot chili **for one**; eat in front of the TV, covered with a heated throw. Sigh frequently, give sullen looks, remark about the certainty of frostbite even though you're indoors, remind spouse that your friend Mary Lou recently moved with her husband, too—to FLORIDA.

Chili cook-off at the Adirondack Park Agency Visitor Interpretive Center, Paul Smiths. Nancie Battaglia

Stage Three—Bargaining

March: If we could just have one spring day I think I might make it. Just one. Really, is that too much to ask for? How about a damned daffodil or two—or hell, how about leaving the house just once without a turtleneck sweater, fleece up to my eyeballs and two pairs of socks? (*Unfortunate stage two regression.*)

Comfort food therapy: Whip up a batch of nachos, make a margarita (or two), and go to a happy tropical place in your mind.

Stage Four—Depression

May through June: Blackfly *season*? Uhh, nooo, it goes like this: spring, summer, fall (I refuse to use the **W** word). This is all just wrong, very sad and very, very wrong. They're already eating fresh tomatoes in Memphis—jerks. (*More unfortunate stage two regression.*)

Comfort food therapy: Consume one stuffed baked potato with enough cheese and sour cream to cause a coronary then drift into a trans-fat-induced coma by 8 p.m. and sleep till noon on Saturday.

Stage Five—Acceptance

September: Moved into our dream home; love the land and our way of life here; NCPR rocks; fall is going to be beautiful; can't wait to see the first snowfall; don't seem to mind the cold so much anymore. What a life!

Comfort food therapy: Fresh shrimp from Larry's fish truck on a bed of salad greens from the Potsdam Food Co-op. Glass of red wine. Eat on the porch and watch the deer wander through the yard.

Naturally cooled hops beverages at snowmobile races at Titus Mountain, Malone. Nancie Battaglia

Sage Bean Soup

1 lb. of great northern beans; soak as directed then cook with 1 large onion, coarsely chopped, a couple of bay leaves and plenty of salt and pepper. Remove bay leaves when beans are fully cooked.

Sauté several shallots, a clove or 2 of fresh garlic, and at least 3 tbsp. of fresh chopped sage in 1 tbsp. of olive oil. Add this to the beans, puree and adjust salt and pepper.

Herb and Cheese Cornbread

2 cups yellow cornmeal

2 eggs

2 cups buttermilk

1 tsp. baking soda

1 tsp. salt

1 tsp. sugar

1 small onion, chopped

¹/₂ cup frozen corn, thawed

1 to 3 tsp. fresh sage, chopped

1 tsp. fresh rosemary and thyme

8 oz. of cheddar cheese, cut into small cubes—do not shred

1 cup butter, melted

Oven to 450°. Combine all ingredients except the butter and mix thoroughly. Melt the butter in an iron skillet and swirl the pan around a bit to completely coat the bottom and sides with butter. Now add the hot butter to the cornmeal mixture and blend thoroughly. Place the mix in your iron skillet and cook for 25 to 35 minutes—until a fork inserted in the center comes out clean. Serve hot.

Both of June's recipes are wheat- and gluten-free.

Survival provisions at Hoss's Country Store, Long Lake. Nancie Battaglia

Winter Festivals, *Lynn Case Ekfelt, Canton (originally published in* Living North Country*)*

Every North Country town has its own mid-February extravaganza with snow-sculpture contests, dogsled races, ice-skating and lots of hearty food. Church basements are filled with people eating ham and scalloped potatoes or chicken and biscuits or turkey with all the trimmings followed by homemade pies. Sometimes we wander among the sculptures at high noon, bundled to the eyebrows against -10° temperatures; sometimes a thaw re-titles every statue "Melting Ice Cream." But at least we're out of the house.

Facing page: *Winter Carnival ice palace, Saranac Lake.* Top: *Tobogganing on Mirror Lake, Lake Placid.* Above left: *Skating, Lake Placid.* Above middle: *Snowshoe adventure, Mount Jo.* Above right: *Peter Roland III licks snowflakes, Saranac Lake.* Nancie Battaglia (5)

Lance Myler is a serious cook. He submitted a copy of his complete cookbook, put together at the request of his family. We selected this vegetarian recipe for its simplicity, accessibility of ingredients and because it's so warmly satisfying on a winter evening.

Cheddar Soup, *Lance Myler, Potsdam*

3 cups diced potatoes

2 large diced carrots

1 large diced onion

2 stalks diced celery

2 tbsp. chicken (or vegetable) base

1 clove garlic, minced

1 tsp. paprika

¹/₂ cup frozen peas

¹/₂ cup flour

1 qt. milk

1 tbsp. butter

1 cup grated cheddar cheese

¹/₂ cup Parmesan cheese

Put diced vegetables in a pot and cover with water. Add chicken or vegetable base, garlic and paprika, and cook until vegetables are tender. Add the frozen peas. Whisk together the flour and milk until smooth. Stir into the vegetable mixture and cook, stirring until thick. Remove from heat. Add the butter and cheese; stir until melted. Do not allow to boil.

Serves 16.

Snow-crusted window at Camp Santanoni, Newcomb. Nancie Battaglia

Coming Home Soup, *Louise Scarlett, Rossie*

*M*y mother, Dorothea Slocum, would have this soup waiting for us whenever we arrived at her home in Rhode Island after a long trip from northern New York. My children grew up on it and look forward to it now when they bring our grandchildren north for a visit. On a recent trip up, our nine-year-old grandson was pleading for a stop at McDonald's. When his mom told him I had Coming Home Soup waiting for him, his response was, "On to Rossie!"

2 tbsp. oil

1 ½ cups chopped leeks (or 2 to 3 cups onions)

2 cups sweet red or green peppers

4 to 6 cloves garlic, chopped

2 to 2 ½ qt. water or chicken stock

2 cups green beans (frozen are fine)

2 cups sliced carrots

4 to 6 cups diced potatoes, skins on (gold or white)

Several large sprigs parsley

2 to 3 tsp. salt

Fresh ground black pepper

½ cup heavy cream

3 tbsp. butter

Sauté leeks (or onions) in the oil until soft then add the garlic and peppers. Add water (or stock), vegetables and seasonings. Bring to a boil then reduce to a simmer. Cook until the vegetables are soft. Add cream. Simmer until warm and swirl in butter to finish.

Serves 8 to 16.

Wild Rice Soup, *George Arnold, Potsdam*

2 tbsp. butter

¼ cup leeks, finely chopped

2 oz. ham, finely chopped

2 tbsp. flour

2 qt. chicken stock

2 cups wild rice

1 cup heavy cream

1 tbsp. parsley, chopped

Salt and pepper

Melt butter in a large pot and cook the leeks until they are soft. Add in the ham and then the flour. Cook over low heat 1 to 2 minutes. Add the stock and rice and simmer until the rice "blooms" (wild rice will swell and burst open). Stir in the cream and chopped parsley, then add salt and pepper, to taste.

Serves 12.

Getting Real about Winter Food

There's something cruel about January 1st being the day we're expected to make good on our resolutions, particularly when the resolutions involve eating less, dieting, cutting back on fat and carbohydrates, all that post-holiday lose-weight thinking. It's winter, for goodness sake. Winter in the North Country. Aren't we supposed to pack on a few pounds? Isn't that the payoff for all that skiing and snowshoeing and scraping off frozen windshields? Big bowls of hot oatmeal laced with maple syrup. Deep soups, robust with onions, squash, corn. Beans, potatoes, pasta, bread.

When we went on air to ask for recipes from listeners, many responded with shameless North Country comfort food ideas. The following recipe reminds me of my old neighbors, Aldena and Milan Conklin, from DeKalb, who made something very similar at least once a week. —ER

Monkey Stew, *Candy Visconti, Chateaugay*

I have wanted to write down the recipe for this comfort food I remember growing up with for a while. It's really a version of shepherd's pie.

Sauté chopped beef with onion and garlic. Add mashed potatoes, whole tomatoes and green string beans in layers, with potatoes on top. Distribute a few pats of butter across the potatoes; sprinkle with paprika and salt. Bake at 350° for 20 to 30 minutes.

Three Sisters Plus a Few Cousins Soup, *Ellen Rocco, DeKalb*

his may be the only dish I make (other than desserts) that does not use garlic. Feel free to add it if you miss that flavor. Please note: amounts are approximate. Add more or less of anything you have a fondness for or have to get rid of.

Enough oil to nicely coat the bottom of your large kettle

2 onions, coarsely diced

2 carrots, sliced

2 stalks celery, sliced

Seasonings to taste (include thyme; oregano—or Italian mixed seasoning; cumin—very important; salt; one small or partial chipotle pepper or a sprinkle of crushed red pepper; a bay leaf; anything else that seems right to you)

8 cups of broth (I use vegetable broth made with bouillon but you could also use chicken stock)

2 cups black beans (from a can or soaked and ready to cook)

1 butternut or comparable winter squash or 2 or 3 yams, peeled and diced

2 cups frozen or fresh corn kernels

Sauté onions, carrots and celery for a few minutes in oiled kettle. Add all seasonings (just a little salt, more can always be added later) and sauté for 1 more minute. Pour in broth, bring to a boil, reduce heat and simmer for about 30 minutes. Add beans (and cook until soft if they are soaked but uncooked). Add squash or yams and corn. Adjust seasoning. Cook gently for another 30 minutes, or longer. Sprinkle a bit of cumin or garam masala or chopped chives or parsley on top of each bowl. Serve with fresh, hot bread.

Serves 6 to 8.

NCPR engineer Radio Bob grills hot dogs on a -5°F day during a station fundraiser. NCPR reporter Jonathan Brown, Canton; Mark Scarlett, Rossie

French-Canadian Meat Pie, *Miriam Kashiwa, Old Forge*

*O*ne of the delectable surprises bequeathed from the Gaspé settlers to our region is this Christmas specialty that our French-Canadian neighbors would share with us. This recipe is from Cecelia Buckley, 95 years old in January 2008.

1 ¼ lbs. ground pork

1 ½ lbs. ground beef

1 ½ lbs. ground veal

1 cup grated and peeled potatoes

½ cup grated onion

3 garlic cloves, minced

1 ½ tsp. salt

½ tsp. pepper

¼ tsp. dried savory

¼ tsp. rubbed sage

⅛ tsp. ground cloves

¼ cup plus 2 tbsp. water (divided)

¼ cup dried breadcrumbs

1 egg

In a large skillet over medium heat, combine and cook the pork, beef, veal, potatoes and onion until the meat is no longer pink. Drain mixture. Stir in the garlic, seasonings and ¼ cup water. Bring to a boil. Reduce heat and simmer for 15 minutes, stirring frequently. Remove from heat; cool to room temperature. Combine egg with 2 tbsp. water in small bowl. Stir breadcrumbs into egg-water. Stir into the meat mixture. Line 9-inch pie plate with bottom pastry; trim even with edge. Fill with meat mixture. Roll out remaining pastry to fit top of pie; place over filling.

Trim, seal and flute edge. Cut slits in pastry. Cover edges of pastry loosely with foil. Bake at 400° for 15 minutes. Remove foil and reduce heat to 375°. Bake 30 to 35 minutes or until crust is golden brown and filling heated through.

Serves 6 to 8.

Donna Mosler keeps smiling and stuffing venison sausage. Robin McClellan, Stockholm

Salt Cod over Potatoes, *Ann Breen Metcalfe, Schroon Lake*

*I*n Schroon Lake from the 1930s through the 1950s, my family's favorite holiday dish was salt codfish. My father was an Irish Roman Catholic, and my Protestant mother had to accommodate her cooking to his many days of abstinence from meat. That was easier said than done in the wintertime Adirondacks, where the only fresh fish came up through a hole in the ice. We were saved by Gorton of Gloucester, which shipped salt codfish in wooden boxes. Mother soaked the fish overnight to get the salt out, then made a white sauce to which, ironically, she added salt. The dish was served piping hot over freshly baked potatoes. We loved it, and sometimes I still make it for Christmas Eve dinner.

Salt codfish

Whole milk as needed

3 tbsp. butter

4 tbsp. flour

Salt, pepper and paprika, to taste

2 large baking potatoes

2 hard-boiled eggs

Soak codfish overnight, changing water at least 3 times. Prick the potato skins and bake them in a 350° oven for 40 minutes. Rinse the salt water off codfish. Cook the fish in gently simmering water until it's easy to flake. Melt butter and add flour to form a roux. Cook 2 to 3 minutes. Wisk in milk as needed to make a thick and smooth sauce, stirring constantly to prevent scorching. Flake the codfish and add it to the sauce. Add salt and pepper. When ready to serve, split the baked potatoes in half and spoon the codfish sauce on top. Decorate with paprika and sliced hard-boiled eggs, and serve. Fresh winter vegetables and a salad add color to the meal.

Serves 4.

Ice fishermen on Upper Saranac Lake. Nancie Battaglia

Pork and Apple Pie, *Jackie Sauter, Canton*

I cooked this dish for Bob when we first met. He loved it. Then we fell in love (love at first bite?) and got married, and I've served it for his birthday every year since. There's something magical about the unique flavor that develops from slow cooking this unusual set of ingredients—perfect for a cold winter's eve.

This recipe takes a while but it's worth it. It can easily be doubled.

2 lbs. boneless pork, trimmed in 1-inch cubes

¼ cup flour

½ tsp. of salt

1 tsp. paprika

6+ tbsp. vegetable oil

1 onion, thinly sliced

1 cup beef or chicken broth

½ cup Madeira

1 ½ cups sliced mushrooms, sautéed in a little butter

2 firm apples

NCPR program director Jackie Sauter and her cousin Cheryl Robinson check on the Thanksgiving Day bird. Radio Bob Sauter, Canton

Combine flour, salt and paprika. Dredge pork cubes in the flour mixture.

Heat 4 tbsp. oil in a large skillet and brown meat on all sides. Remove meat from skillet and place in a 2-qt. casserole. Add remaining 2 or so tbsp. of oil to the skillet and sauté the sliced onion and sliced mushrooms until soft and slightly browned. Sprinkle remaining flour mixture over onion and mushrooms and cook for 2 more minutes. Add broth and Madeira. Bring to a boil, then turn down heat and stir for a few minutes, until thickened. Pour into casserole with the meat. Cover and bake in 325° oven about 90 minutes, or until the meat is fork-tender. Cool and skim off extra fat. Dice the apples and stir into the meat mixture.

Roll out a pastry crust and cover top of the casserole dish. Bake at 400° for about 30 minutes or until crust is nicely browned.

VARIATION #1: Instead of standard pastry crust, top casserole with mashed potatoes, to which a ½ cup of flour has been added.

VARIATION #2: Never mind the crust. Just serve it as a stew with mashed potatoes and a nice ale. Happy Birthday, Bob!

Radio Bob's Pork Chop Casserole (thanks, Mom), *Radio Bob Sauter, Canton*

This is the only thing I can cook that involves more than a single ingredient (like steak, for example). This is my recipe:

1) Preheat oven to 350°.

2) Brown up some (6 in this case) pork chops in a pan on high-ish heat. You can calculate 2 chops per hungry individual, 1 per normal person. Use loin chops or equivalent, with the bone in place—and some fat left on.

3) Slice up a big onion. I like those mild purple ones. The slices should be about $1/4$-inch thick.

4) Open 2 cans of Campbell's Cream of Mushroom Soup and 1 can of Campbell's Golden Mushroom Soup.

Radio Bob continues a tradition of eating hot peppers on the fundraiser-week edition of his R&B show. Peppers provided for more than two decades by Andrea "Hot Mama" Bellinger, of Ogdensburg. NCPR reporter David Sommerstein, Canton

5) Empty one of the Cream of Mushroom cans into the bottom of a casserole dish (8- to 12-inch round, with a top), then put in about $1/4$ of the onion, then 2 or so of the browned chops, then a can of Golden Mushroom, more onion, 2 more chops, etc. Finish off with more Cream of Mushroom Soup.

6) Cover and put in oven for 1 $1/2$ hours. (To avoid boil-over spills, put some foil or a cookie sheet under the casserole.)

7) When it's almost done, cook up a small box of Minute Rice … this is easy and fun. Bring 2 cups of water to a boil and stir in 3 cups of rice, turn off the heat and cover (stirring occasionally). It's best to make a whole box so you don't have to figure out what to do with extra rice, but if you do less, measure the amount of rice first, so you can use the correct amount of water.

8) As a great side dish, put some applesauce into a saucepan, and add too much cinnamon. You'll know when you've added too much because everyone around you will say, "That's too much!" But this is important, too little spoils the effect. Anyway, warm up the applesauce and cinnamon.

9) Call everyone to dinner, spoon gravy from casserole on rice and pork chops. Applesauce can be next to other ingredients on the plates.

10) Leftovers of this are also great.

Serves 3 to 4.

Lentil and Sausage Stew, *Carol Berard, Canton*

T*he ingredients for this recipe can be* (more or less) *increased or decreased depending on your taste.*

¹/₂ stick of kielbasa, sweet or hot sausage sliced in ¹/₄- to ¹/₂-inch rounds

1 cup orange or French green lentils

3 or 4 shallots, sliced

1 medium onion or several leeks, sliced

5 or 6 garlic cloves

4 to 6 medium potatoes

4 to 6 oz. white mushrooms, halved then quartered

4 to 6 medium carrots, sliced

1 to 2 celery sticks, sliced

About 6 cups of liquid (chicken or vegetable stock), amount will be determined by the amount of solid ingredients you add

1 tsp. of dried thyme (more if fresh; also, if fresh, just add the leaves)

Salt and pepper, to taste

Bunch of Swiss chard, kale or spinach (chard and kale, stems included, will need to be sliced)

Fresh parsley and/or cilantro chopped to be added in last minute of cooking

(For a sweeter-flavored stew you might add parsnips, sweet potatoes and apricots.)

Spice mix:

1 tbsp. more or less of cumin

1 tsp. more or less of paprika

¹/₂ tsp. more or less of cayenne red pepper

¹/₂ tsp. of turmeric

In a Dutch oven, brown sausage in 1 to 2 tbsp. of olive oil being careful not to burn. Remove sausage from pan and drain on paper towel. Set aside. Next, add more olive oil to pan, loosen the browned sausage bits stuck to the pan so they won't burn and, in pan, sauté (in this order) shallots, onions till translucent, carrots and celery, mushrooms and garlic. Now add a little more oil; then add lentils and potatoes. Sauté for a few more minutes. While that's sautéing, warm the cumin, paprika, cayenne red pepper and turmeric in a small pan for just a few seconds stirring constantly, do not let burn. Add the warmed spices, thyme and sausage to the sauté pan. Mix until combined, then add liquid. (If you heat the liquid separately and then add it to the vegetable mix it will start cooking right away.) Bring mixture just to a boil, turn down the heat and simmer covered for 30 to 45 minutes. During the last 10 to 15 minutes, stir in the Swiss chard or other greens. Continue cooking until the greens are tender.

To thicken the stew you could make a roux in a separate small skillet with 2 tbsp. of butter and 2 tbsp. of flour and 1 cup of stock. Add this to the stew, stir in and continue to cook for a few more minutes and then serve, either stirring the parsley and cilantro into the stew mixture or sprinkling on top of individual bowls.

I Follow Directions, *Shelley Pike, Canton*

When I cook for myself, I rummage through the fridge, find anything that could possibly go together, add spices from my meager spice collection, heat the oven to 375° (a nice, safe number), and away we go. When I'm cooking for others, I reach for my trusty ring-bound Better Homes & Gardens Cookbook and follow the instructions to the letter. If the book tells me to jump up and down three times before putting an uncooked creation in the oven, I do it. I figure that if it works for them, it'll work for me.

Note from Chef George: On cooking with and without a recipe. When I was 10 years old, I had a John Nagy® paint-by-numbers set that helped me to produce some attractive pictures. My mother often would frame and hang my masterpieces out of a sense of maternal loyalty, no doubt. However, no one—not even my own mother—confused the outcome of this process with great art.

In a similar manner, no one will ever become a great cook just by following recipes, despite the fact that they will complete some tasty dishes.

To a novice cook, a recipe is an instruction manual that must be followed step by step until completion; but to an experienced cook a recipe is a general blueprint that suggests a combination of ingredients be acted on by a number of culinary processes. An experienced cook feels confident with substituting ingredients, adding new ingredients and modifying the procedures.

The experienced cook knows all the proper culinary techniques (braising, sautéing, broiling, etc.), understands the essential nature of a wide variety of ingredients and knows from experience how one ingredient will react with another. If you have creativity and an exceptional palate you may eventually become a great cook. But this will never happen by just following recipes.

Now baking—that's a different matter! Cooking is art but baking is science. Of course there is room for creativity in baking as well, but the basic ratios of ingredients must be followed or your project is doomed.

Cooking? A succinct opinion. Alan Tuttle, Oxbow

Harbor Inn House Meatloaf, *Roger and Vicki Hyde, Clayton*

5 lbs. ground beef

4 cups onion, minced

2 1/2 cups celery, minced

1 1/2 peppers, diced

2 tbsp. oil

Salt and pepper, to taste

3 tbsp. basil

1 tbsp. oregano

2 tbsp. balsamic vinegar

2 tbsp. Worcestershire sauce

2 tbsp. A1 Steak Sauce

1 bottle ketchup

2 cups breadcrumbs

1 cup oatmeal

Sauté ground beef, onion, celery and peppers in oil until tender. Season with salt and pepper, basil, oregano, balsamic vinegar, Worcestershire sauce, A1 sauce and 1/2 bottle of ketchup. Mix in breadcrumbs and oatmeal. Make up 4 equal loaves and shape like bread. Cook and taste for seasoning.

Top each loaf with the remaining 1/2 bottle of ketchup diluted with water. Place the loaf pans in a 2-inch hotel pan and set in a 400° oven. Create a water bath in the hotel pan (1/3 full). Bake the meat loaf until it is 150° internal temperature. Cool, remove from pans, wrap and chill or freeze. Each loaf provides 3 portions for dinner and 4 portions for lunch.

Serves 16.

Rustic camp après-dinner conversation, St. Huberts. Nancie Battaglia

Aged Venison, *Chase Twichell, Keene*

One Christmas Eve when I was about 10 and my sister eight, one of our dinner guests insisted on bringing the meat. This was Adrian Edmonds, who was famous in Keene Valley for his knowledge of the woods and for his storytelling and his jokes. What he brought was a haunch of venison. Adrian had aged it in his garage, and my sister and I thought the meat looked disgusting.

My mother, who was an excellent cook, made off with it to the kitchen while Adrian told us the story of how he'd shot the deer (which involved hand-to-paw combat with a bear and dragging the carcass on a litter of balsam boughs from the top of Giant Mountain down to the valley). When the meat appeared on the table, it looked like any other roast, and after a few reluctant, tiny bites, we demolished what was on our plates. To this day, I remember the utterly distinctive flavor and texture, and I have never since had venison of that quality. My sister, too, agrees that it was the best meal we ever had. Before he died some years ago, I mentioned that night to Adrian and thanked him for the memory and the tall tales. "The part about the bear was true," he said.

Robert Buck (left) and Lloyd Duso with successful deer harvest at the Outlet Club hunting camp, Tupper Lake. Photograph courtesy of Lloyd Duso

Greek Burgers, *Lynn Case Ekfelt, Canton*

*O*n our first date 24 years ago, my now-husband Nils invited me over for dinner. The main dish was a recipe he'd invented after eating in a Greek restaurant and liking the spices he had tasted. One bite of those burgers and I decided anyone who could cook like that was a keeper. Now Greek burgers are our standard anniversary dinner—made with our own home-grown mint.

1 lb. ground chuck

1 medium onion, chopped fine

3 large cloves garlic, minced

³/₄ tsp. cumin

¹/₂ tsp. cinnamon

¹/₄ tsp. cloves

1 tsp. oregano

10 twists fresh ground black pepper

¹/₂ tsp. salt

1 cup plain yogurt

1 tsp. dried mint, crumbled, or 8 leaves fresh mint, chopped

Mix the meat, onion, garlic and spices; form into patties. Pan-broil the patties in a hot skillet for 5 minutes per side. Serve topped with a sauce made by mixing the yogurt and mint.

Serves 4.

Michele caught this 10 lb. northern pike in February on the St. Lawrence River; the next day, it helped her win First Place People's Choice Award in the Morristown Chili/Chowder Cook-Off. Michele Whalen, Morristown

The Jackrabbit Trail between Saranac Lake and Lake Placid. Nancie Battaglia

Lamb and Cabbage Casserole, *Connie Meng, Canton*

*A*t one point in my peripatetic life I was engaged to a Norwegian, so I thought it behooved me to learn to make one of his favorite national dishes. I did, and it's now become one of my family's favorite winter comfort meals.

2 tbsp. vegetable oil

1 ½ cups sliced onions

3 to 4 lbs. shoulder lamb chops, chopped into 2-inch pieces

2 tbsp. salt

2 ½ cups beef stock or bouillon

⅓ cup flour

2 tbsp. whole black peppercorns, tied in cheesecloth and lightly bruised with a rolling pin

2 lbs. cabbage, cut into wedges

1 cup chopped celery

Preheat oven to 350°. Heat oil in heavy skillet. Add meat and turn until lightly browned. With tongs transfer meat to large mixing bowl. Sprinkle with flour and toss with wooden spoons till meat is coated and flour is gone. Set skillet aside.

In 5- to 6-qt. casserole with a lid or a Dutch oven, arrange layer of meat, then cabbage. Sprinkle with half the celery and half the onions and salt lightly. Repeat, ending with vegetables. Pour off most of the fat from the skillet and deglaze it by pouring in the stock and stirring over high heat, scraping up any browned bits. Pour over casserole. Add bag of peppercorns, cover and bake for 1 ½ to 2 hours—until meat is tender when pierced with a knife.

Serves 16.

Late winter season's greeting, Titus Mountain, Malone. Nancie Battaglia

Pot Pourri, *Mildred "Noonie" Burns Dechene, Long Lake*

*M*y mother, Elsie Stanton Burns, heard this recipe on the radio during the Depression. It's great any time of year, but it is especially good for a cold winter supper. (I think it's even better if it is refrigerated for a day or two.) "Pot" is pronounced "pō."

1 lb. ground beef

3 onions, sliced

¹/₃ cup barley

1 ¹/₂ qt. water

1 qt. canned tomatoes

3 carrots, sliced

3 potatoes, diced

3 stalks celery, diced

1 tsp. each of A1 Steak Sauce, Worcestershire sauce and paprika

1 tsp. salt and pepper

In a 3 ¹/₂- to 4-qt. kettle, cook ground beef gently (browned). Add onion. Cover. Cook 3 minutes. Then add barley, tomatoes, water, salt and pepper. Cover and simmer gently for 1 hour.

Add vegetables, sauces and paprika. Cover and simmer gently 1 hour longer (stir occasionally). I use tomato juice instead of canned tomatoes and don't add salt.

Serves 8.

Even bobcats have to eat. After 50 years of watching birds at feeders outside their window, this was the first bobcat ever spotted by the LeFebvres. Gary and Mary LeFebvre, Onchiota

Note from Chef George: One of the things I love about pasta is that it is so adaptable to the seasons. A light primavera in the spring works just fine, but so does a rich and heavy pasta dish in the winter, if you punch up the flavor and add a bit more cheese to make it satisfying on a cold night. A perfect way to prepare pasta this time of year is to make a pasta bake. Sautéed meats and vegetables blended with al dente pasta and cheese then baked until it's bubbling and brown, paired with a green salad, makes a wonderful Sunday night dinner. My favorite Simple Sunday Winter Pasta Bake uses penne, or any other pasta easy to eat with a fork, cooked al dente. After draining the pasta put it back in the same pot with some sauce and simmer to let the sauce soak into the pasta. In another pan sauté artichoke hearts, mushrooms, garlic and slices of sun-dried tomatoes. Add this to the pasta. Put all into a casserole dish and dot with ricotta cheese that has been seasoned with chopped herbs, salt and pepper. Sprinkle shredded mozzarella and grated Parmesan over the top. Finish with seasoned breadcrumbs that have been blended with a bit of olive oil and bake until the top is nicely browned.

Knoble's Knoodles: Rustic Knoodles for a Quantum Age, *Bill Knoble,*
Chestertown and DeKalb

This recipe is courtesy of my grandmother from Eagle Grove, Iowa, daughter of a Swedish immigrant, who, visiting in 1950, made egg noodles for a stewed chicken dinner. These noodles have substance, flavor, and are so lacking in uniformity that there is no confusing them with their buddies from the supermarket. They are at home in stews, spaghetti dishes or soups. Her method as remembered by a then five-year-old:

For every egg used add water from half of the broken eggshell. Add flour. Add salt. Roll out and cut into noodles. Four to 6 eggs makes oodles of noodles.

Here's that recipe again for those unfamiliar with measuring with eggshells:

Break 4 to 6 eggs into a measuring cup and add half as much cold water as there is egg. Add salt to the tune of 1 $^1/_2$ to 2 tsp. per egg used. Mix. Add flour until the dough is stiff enough to roll with resistance. OPTIONAL: to the egg mix add spices (dill, thyme, black pepper), chives, dry cheese, bits of olive, hot pepper, (be inventive) and then the flour.

Roll out the dough as thin as possible on a large flat, floured surface. It's handy to let the rolled-out dough slide over the edge of the counter to help stretch it. Flour and then fold the dough to make noodles. Slicing with a heavy cleaver or carving knife makes the job easier. The noodles are best when cooked in boiling water directly after slicing. If they can't all be used, freeze them on a cookie sheet, then store them in plastic bags. They can be dried, but that increases cooking time and the net result is a noodle with a slightly mummified center.

Christmas Ravioli, *Anne Garbarino, Eagle Bay*

This is a family recipe, brought when the Garbarino family came to America from the mountains of northern Italy, in 1914. When making this recipe, my husband uses a special rolling pin with forms for the ravioli. His mother had it made for him by a man in Boonville.

Pasta dough:

6 cups of flour, we mix semolina with white flour

6 eggs

6 eggshell halves filled with water

Filling:

2 onions, chopped

1 clove of garlic, chopped

1 bag of spinach or Swiss chard

¹/₄ lb. Genoa salami

1 egg

¹/₄ cup breadcrumbs

Louis Garbarino shaping ravioli, Eagle Bay.
Anne Garbarino, Eagle Bay

Sauté onion and garlic in frying pan. Cook Swiss chard. In a food processor (or a grinder), grind up the onion mixture, spinach and the Genoa salami. Mix with an egg and breadcrumbs to hold it together.

Make a hole in the center of the flour. Place eggs in the hole and scramble them. Then add the water and mix the eggs, water and flour together. You may need to add some water. When it is mixed, knead the dough to get it to stick together. Use some flour—but not too much—on your kneading board. When finished, put the dough back into the bowl to rest. (My husband, Louis, says this resting was to allow his grandmother time to go to church on Sunday morning.)

When you come back to the dough, take a part of it (divide dough into 4ths or so) and roll it out on a board. Or use a pasta machine. When the pasta is thin enough for you, spread the filling very thinly onto half of the dough. Then fold over the other half of the dough. Now use the fancy rolling pin to mark the pasta dough into squares. If you don't have a special rolling pin, use a pizza cutter to cut the pasta dough into squares. Once you fill the ravioli, you have to crimp the edges with a fork to seal the pasta squares. If you don't the filling may come out when you boil the dough. Let the pasta dry (about an hour) until you are ready to cook the ravioli. Or freeze the ravioli on a cookie sheet to use another day. Put into freezer bags when they are frozen.

Top with any sauce you like. I don't put much meat in mine, since the ravioli are rather filling.

Serves 12.

Pasta Con Pepperoni Fritti, *Libby and Dennie Brandt, Canton*

*T*he sabbatical year we lived in Genoa we became addicted to Italian food and cooking with seasonal ingredients. Wednesdays and Saturdays are now our special Italian nights, and North Country Public Radio is definitely involved. For Wednesdays, we tape Car Talk. On Saturdays, A Prairie Home Companion accompanies our cooking and feasting.

1 red pepper, sliced

1 green pepper, sliced

1 yellow pepper, sliced

Olive oil

4 garlic cloves, chopped

1 tbsp. capers

10 calamata olives, sliced

1 anchovy filet, soaked in milk, then chopped

Salt and pepper

Parsley, chopped

Gently fry the peppers in olive oil along with the garlic for about 10 minutes. Add the capers, calamata olives and anchovy. Salt and pepper, to taste. Add a handful of chopped parsley.

Serve with grated Parmesan over pasta of choice. Recipe is easily doubled.

Serves 2.

Note from Chef George: For a vegetarian twist, omit the anchovy but add finely chopped mushrooms when you are frying the peppers and garlic and add a dash of soy sauce. This (mushroom and soy sauce) will provide a similar depth of flavor.

Pasta challenge at Nicola's, Lake Placid.
Nancie Battaglia

Ice Storm '98 Stew

It is not paranoia if the event can—and does—happen. From my earliest years in the North Country, I insisted on having wood heat and on retaining access to an old dug well (just throw a bucket in and you have water—without electricity). My neighbors, Aldena and Milan, taught me this: count on it, the power will go out—for a few hours or a few days, on a regular basis. In January 1998, during the great Northeast ice storm, we were without electricity for three weeks. We were OK—heat and water available (humph, like I said, not paranoia). Keeping food frozen would have worked using the back porch, if the weather hadn't fluctuated during the first few days after the storm. So, when the ice crystals in the meat and vegetables started to soften, I dumped everything from my freezer into a couple of huge kettles, threw in some potatoes, onions, garlic and seasonings, and stewed it all up on the wood cookstove. Later that day Clyde Morse, the DeKalb road supervisor, clumped into the house and told me the crew was going to try to clear trees from the two or three miles of road just beyond my house, still impassable. I invited him to bring everyone back for ice-storm stew. That evening, with candles and kerosene lighting the kitchen, half-a-dozen tired, cold men piled in around the table and ate a lot of my stew. But not all of it. Next day, I brought the leftovers into work to feed staff and volunteers running the *generator-powered station. One colleague, who ate two bowls of the ice-storm stew, left me a message: "Please, Ellen, this is the best stew I've ever had. Can you give me the recipe?" My answer: "Begin with a power outage. Then dump everything in your freezer together and cook until done." —ER*

Power Outage Macaroni and Cheese, *Susan Sweeney Smith, Cranberry Lake*

We have a lot of power outages in Cranberry Lake, with at least one 48-hour outage each year. Our generator won't run the whole house, so refrigerators and freezers become a challenge pretty quickly. Day two, I start to run out of energy and make a special dish using up all the hard cheese, milk and fresh vegetables in the fridge. If we get as far as day three, I head to a hotel with a restaurant.

However many 8-oz. blocks of cheese I have on hand (don't use the horseradish cheese that you love but your family hates unless you want to eat the whole casserole yourself), cut into small blocks

1 1/2 cups of milk per block of cheese (I have "used up" heavy cream in this as well)

1/4 cup butter or margarine (tastes so much better with butter)

1 to 1 1/2 cups of macaroni (any pasta but spaghetti and derivations thereof will work) per block of cheese

1/2 tsp. salt

1/4 tsp. pepper

1/4 cup all-purpose flour

Vegetables of all sorts, chopped small (use your discretion here: rutabaga and parsnips aren't great in this context, but onions, peppers, tomatoes, green beans and mushrooms are fine)

Cook macaroni.

Cook the vegetables in small amounts of butter or light oil until soft. Cook to the crispness you prefer. If you are using tomatoes, cook most of the water off.

Cook and stir butter or margarine, salt and pepper over medium heat until butter is melted. Stir in flour. Cook over low heat until mixture is smooth and bubbly. Remove from heat. Stir in milk. Heat to boiling, stirring constantly. Boil and stir for 1 minute. Remove from heat. Stir in cheese until melted.

Place macaroni in a buttered casserole dish, add vegetables and cheese mixture. Stir well and cover.

If your oven works, bake for 30 minutes at 375°. On the occasion when the oven isn't working, I wrap the casserole in heavy towels to keep heat in and let sit for 20 minutes or so. It's a bit runnier in the serving but still tastes fine.

I am usually serving teenagers and friends and I estimate 1 block of cheese per kid. If no teenagers, a 1-block of cheese version serves 3 or 4 adults.

The Crested Hens and the Potluck

You know you're city born and bred when you've never been to a potluck. This cultural gap may be changing nowadays, but when I was growing up, I thought of potlucks as something quaint that hillbillies engaged in. I want to tell you that I am now a potluck devotee. I've been converted, brothers and sisters. I believe the potluck brings together friends and neighbors like nothing else—particularly in the dark days of winter. My neighbors will tell you that I am always finding excuses to organize a potluck—the first snow-

Crested Hens Martha Gallagher, left, and Julie Robards jammin' … the strawberry variety, in a High Peaks kitchen. Nancie Battaglia

fall, the last snowfall, the biggest snowfall, the hens are laying again, it's Sunday, it's Tuesday, let's use up holiday leftovers—heck, just fill in the blank and have a potluck.

While we were putting this food book together, Julie Robards contacted me about the Crested Hens, a group of friends in the High Peaks area who "appreciate food, wine, art, music and the companionship of each other." An eclectic bunch—each with a food specialty, all seemingly talented in a variety of ways—sharing monthly meals to celebrate birthdays and other occasions. I think of the Crested Hens as the top shelf of the potluck circuit.

Some of the memorable recipes from the last year, according to Julie:

Nan's Pumpkin Soup and her Sausage Soup with Homemade Gnocchi;

Amy's Salmon with Dill Sauce; Martha's Scotch Eggs; Barb's

Incredible Butternut Squash Salad with Hazelnut Dressing and Cold

Potato Soup garnished with beautiful nasturtiums; Kay's Basmati

Rice; Martha Gallagher's Parsnip and Carrot Sauté; Mary's Divine

Chocolate Decadence Cake; Wendy's Chocolate Yule Log with

Meringue Mushrooms; and Elly's Beet Gnocchi. —ER

This dessert comes from one of the card-carrying Crested Hens:

Divine Decadence Chocolate Cake, *Mary Valley, Wilmington*

The only tradition with this recipe is to share it. Everyone asks for the recipe because they love it so. It's simple to assemble and makes a beautiful presentation.

¹/₂ cup light or dark corn syrup

3 eggs

¹/₂ cup butter

1 tsp. vanilla

6 squares (6 oz.) semisweet chocolate

1 cup unsifted flour

³/₄ cup sugar

1 cup chopped walnuts

In a large saucepan, bring corn syrup and butter to a boil, stirring occasionally. Remove from heat. Add chocolate; stir until melted. Add sugar, stir in eggs, one at a time, then vanilla, flour and nuts.

Pour into a greased and floured 9-inch layer cake pan. Bake at 350° for about 30 minutes or until cake tester inserted in center comes out clean. Cool in pan 10 minutes; cool completely on rack. Prepare glaze; pour on top and sides. Let stand 1 hour.

Chocolate Glaze:
In small saucepan, melt 3 squares (3 oz.) semisweet chocolate with 1 tbsp. butter over low heat, stirring often. Remove from heat. Stir in 2 tbsp. corn syrup and 1 tsp. milk.

You may artfully arrange fresh berries on the top. I prefer raspberries.

Serves 10 to 12.

Fruit Pizza, *Jackie Sauter, Canton*

*T*his is an easy dessert to prepare and decorating it can be lots of fun. This recipe can easily be doubled for a larger pan or rimmed cookie sheet.

Crust:

³/₄ cup butter

¹/₂ cup powdered sugar

1 ¹/₂ cups flour

Preheat oven to 350°.

Mix butter, sugar and flour until crumbly. Pat into a 12-inch pizza pan and bake at 350° for 10 to 15 minutes, until just slightly browned. Cool in pan.

Topping:

8 oz. cream cheese, at room temperature

¹/₂ cup sugar

1 tsp. vanilla

Mix cream cheese, sugar and vanilla until well blended. Spread over cooled crust in pan.

Glaze:

2 tbsp. cornstarch

1 cup water or light-colored apple juice

1 tsp. lemon juice

¹/₂ cup sugar

Mix the cornstarch with a few tbsp. of the water or juice and set aside.

Pour the rest of water or juice in a saucepan; add lemon juice and sugar. Heat; stir in cornstarch mixture, blending well. Let it boil a few minutes until it thickens and turns clear, stirring frequently. Turn off heat and let glaze cool.

Fruit:

Select a variety of fruit (sliced strawberries, bananas, kiwis, drained mandarin oranges, etc.) and arrange decoratively over the topping. You can spread fruit randomly, in a decorative pattern, paint a picture or spell out words, or use green and red fruit for a Christmas dessert.

Tip: Be sure your fruit is well drained so the liquid doesn't run or discolor the pizza.

Spoon warm (not hot) glaze over fruit. The glaze is important because it adds sweetness to the fruit and prevents if from discoloring. It also gives the pizza a more elegant look. After glazing, refrigerate pizza until set. Cut into slices.

Adirondack Honey and Dried Fruit Tart, *David Tomberlin, Tupper Lake*

1 rolled pie crust

1 jar Walnuts in Buckwheat Honey (available from The Well Dressed Food Company, or mix a cup of walnuts with a ¹/₄ cup of your favorite local honey)

¹/₂ cup light brown sugar

¹/₂ stick unsalted butter

1 cup roughly chopped dried apricots

¹/₂ cup chopped dried dates

¹/₂ cup roughly chopped dried mission figs

2 cups Adirondack Crunchy Granola (available from The Well Dressed Food Company, or use your favorite granola)

¹/₂ cup half-and-half

Preheat oven to 450°. Line a 9-inch tart shell with pie crust. Prick all over with a fork and bake for 10 to 12 minutes.

Reduce oven to 350°. Combine the walnuts, sugar and butter in a heavy saucepan and bring to a boil; boil for a minute and remove from heat. Mix in remaining ingredients and allow to cool for 5 minutes. Transfer mixture to pie shell and bake for 30 minutes. Allow to cool for an hour before serving. Ideal with French vanilla ice cream.

Orange Muffins, *Rosalie Smith, Massena*

M*aking and sharing muffins is a tradition I learned from my mother. She always had muffins when I went to visit her and she would give me some to bring home. The orange-bran muffins are a recipe from* The Clan MacLeod Society of Glengarry Cookbook. *My maternal grandmother was from Glengarry, Ontario.*

5 eggs

3 cups white sugar

1 ¹/₄ cups vegetable oil

3 seedless oranges, not peeled, cut into quarters, chopped in a blender (adding some of the buttermilk helps blend the oranges smoothly)

2 cups raisins

1 qt. buttermilk

4 cups flour

3 tsp. baking soda

2 cups All-Bran Cereal

4 cups Bran Flakes Cereal

In a large bowl, mix first 7 ingredients together. Then stir in last 4 ingredients. Cover and refrigerate for at least a day. May be stored for up to 2 to 3 weeks and used in small batches. Bake at 375° for 25 minutes in greased muffin pans.

For a number of years, Rosalie and Bruce Smith volunteered at North Country Public Radio as readers for our service for the sight-impaired. Rosalie never arrived empty-handed. The muffins were always gone before the workday was over.

The Holidays, *Martha Foley, Canton*

I think of the time between Thanksgiving and Christmas as one long fugue, melding old habits and traditions with new. It starts with an inner monologue of lists: of people, places, things to do, things to make, things to buy, events to mark on the calendar. I'm an editor, so while in the beginning the monologue grows more and more complex and detailed, it gets simpler again as deadlines approach.

The annual eggnog party is one of those deadlines. It comes before Christmas, but as close to Christmas Eve as possible. The guest list includes neighbors who are close by and close friends. Sometimes just a few people turn up; sometimes there's barely room to raise a glass. Come to think of it, it always *used* to be just a few people, and we were pretty much all the same age. But the center of our own extended families has migrated—now we're pretty much it. There are precious few in the generation before us, and more and more grown kids—boyfriends and girlfriends, brides and grooms—fill the room.

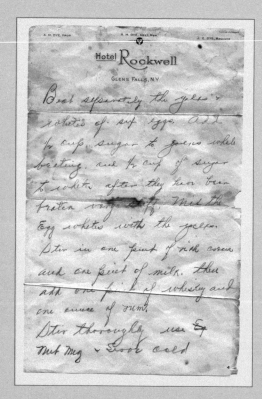

This recipe, as well as the Christmas Eve tradition, is credited to my grandfather, John Elmer Dye, a Hoosier who settled in Charlotte, North Carolina. The story is from my mother, who grew up there in the teens and '20s.

They served eggnog to their friends on Christmas Eve, too. But in their neighborhood, it was a sort of rotating open house. You might be at your neighbors' house, while they were back at yours. I like our way better.

Here are a couple of my favorite hoiliday recipes:

Martha's Family Eggnog

W e like to mix eggnog with applejack, but my grandfather, a Southerner, spiked his with plenty of bourbon.

6 eggs

1 cup sugar

1 pt. heavy cream

1 pt. milk

Grated nutmeg

Separate eggs. Beat whites till fairly stiff (creamy) adding $1/2$ cup sugar. Beat yolks, adding $1/2$ cup sugar—they will also be creamy, like soft butter. Fold together. Stir in cream and milk. Add nutmeg, to taste. Voilà!

Anne M. Dye's Pulled Mints

2 cups sugar

1 cup water

Butter the size of an egg (Anne Dye cut about an $1/8$-inch slice from a lb. of butter)

Peppermint oil

Cook until it makes a ball when tested in cold water.

Empty onto cold marble, or something like that, cold. Add 5 drops of peppermint oil.

As soon as you can stand the heat, start "pulling." First fold the edges into the middle to make a blob, then get working—pull and fold continually. The creaminess is determined by the pulling. You need to start when it's still SO hot. Some people use rubber gloves.

Then twist into strings the size of your thumb and cut with scissors into bite-sized lengths to suit. Let the pieces dry in place. When they've hardened put them in a tin and shake hard.

Sugar Cookies: Tradition

Part 1, *Jan Hutslar, Hermon*

This is a story of a ritual, now a tradition. Sugar cookies are how it started: plain white dough rolled thin and cut with my grandmother's cookie cutters—bell, star, tree, angel, wreath. The entire family sat around the kitchen table, each with a personal square of wax paper—our canvas—where we turned plain cookies into works of art. Or, into disgustingly sweet mounds of frosting and sprinkles, depending on our age and aesthetic sensibility.

Holiday cookie walk magic, Adirondack Community Church, and Ellen Lansing's third birthday, Lake Placid. Nancie Battaglia

Mom did the cutting and baking—shoveling mountains of cooled shapes into the middle of the table. We five children were the artists. There were bowls of butter frosting—blue, red, green, yellow and white—and sprinkles, raisins, coconut, pecans, and our favorites—the red hots and little silver balls. It went on all day, starting out with strong, creative energy, making a perfect tree and pointing out its beauty to anyone who would look. By the last tray, we slathered frosting and moved on.

The colorful cookies were stacked between sheets of wax paper in Mom's huge turkey roasting pan. Aside from the occasional cookie we had the courage to sneak when Mom wasn't looking, they were saved for the many holiday gatherings of family and friends, artfully arranged on fine trays.

The tradition continues.

Each Christmas, each generation, sugar cookies are baked, decorated and eaten.

Part 2, *Maggie Hutslar Wood, Hermon*

We wake early. We mix the frosting and sugar, the vibrant colors matching our moods today. We roll out three kinds of cookie dough—vanilla, chocolate and gingerbread, and then cut the first cookies, bringing our assortment of cookie cutters.

There are the normal ones, of course, ones you'd expect, some from my great-grandmother: angels, bells, stars, gingerbread men and so on. Then there are the strange and less conventional: the hand, squirrel, dragonfly, pig. As we put the first batch of cookies into the oven, people begin to arrive. Since most of our family lives so far away, these visitors are our close friends, our northern family. We begin to decorate cookies, our finished products ranging from my mom's gorgeous edible art to my stepsister's "prisoner gingerbread man" complete with a ball and chain made from an M&M and some coconut.

By the end of the day we're tired and full of sugar from all the frosting we just couldn't resist. We pack the cookies between sheets of wax paper in decorative tins—a tin for each person. Interesting and eccentric cookies for holiday parties in many houses.

Holiday cookie walk grab, Adirondack Community Church, Lake Placid.
Nancie Battaglia

Butter or Sugar Cookies, *Bill Knoble, Chestertown and DeKalb*

Cookies: butter or sugar? Originally from a recipe from our next-door neighbor in Kirtland Hills, Ohio, Mary Wolff, who made those squished-out-of-a-tube fancy cookies with this recipe. The method I prefer makes an understated, plain cookie that's like a really good joke that takes a while for the laughter to set in. The dough is shaped into a fat salami, wrapped in wax paper, refrigerated, then sliced about ³/₁₆ of an inch and cooked on a sheet until the edges are just turning tan.

1 lb. cultured, lightly salted butter

1 ³/₄ cups sugar

4 cups flour

1 egg

1 tbsp. vanilla extract

1 ¹/₂ tbsp. Jack Daniel's Whiskey (or brandy, rum, scotch)

Salt, to taste

Bake in moderate oven and pay attention! As soon as the edges turn tan, pull the cookies out of the oven, remove from sheet and cool on newspapers.

Easy Icing for Cookie Decorating, *Ellen Rocco, DeKalb*

1 cup confectioners' sugar

2 tsp. milk

2 tsp. light corn syrup

¹/₄ tsp. liquid flavoring (vanilla or almond)

Assorted food coloring

In a small bowl stir together sugar and milk until smooth, then beat in corn syrup and flavoring. Add a bit more corn syrup if icing is too thick; add a bit more sugar if too thin. Divide into separate bowls for each color you plan to use. Add food coloring. Cookies may be painted with a brush or simply dipped into icing.

Maggie Wood Hutslar and Jay Van de Water, Colton.
Photographer unknown

Cookie Exchange, *Lyn Burkett, Potsdam*

When I was in fourth grade, I told my mother in early December that I wanted to have a cookie exchange party for my friends. Each guest brought a shoebox with enough of her favorite cookies to share, as well as copies of the recipes. I still have those recipes in my friends' 10-year-old handwriting. Now, more than 30 years later, I've returned to hosting the cookie exchange. The rules are similar: each guest brings three dozen of his or her favorite cookies to trade. We all sample the cookies, and everyone introduces themselves and their cookies. The party is just as much fun now as it was when I was 10 years old.

Molasses Cookies, *Mary-Ann Cateforis, Potsdam*

I have fond memories of driving out to Stanley Northrop's farm outside of Potsdam in the 1970s with my clean glass jar and visiting a while before coming home with a gallon of cold, fresh-from-the-cow, unpasteurized, un-homogenized milk. I made yogurt from that milk, and we all drank the milk raw. Stanley knew everything anyone needed to know about producing clean, safe milk. For a number of years a batch of these cookies was my Christmas present to the Northrop family. The recipe originally came from Veneita Need Wells, of one of the old Potsdam-area Thompson farm families. I don't know how far back the recipe goes.

1 cup butter

1 ¹/₃ cups sugar

2 cups molasses, unsulfured

2 tbsp. apple cider vinegar

7 cups flour

1 tbsp. ginger, ground

1 tbsp. cinnamon

1 tsp. cloves, ground

4 tsp. baking soda

2 eggs

²/₃ cup water

Melt butter in a large enamel pan and stir in sugar. Add molasses and vinegar. In bowl, sift together flour, spices and baking soda. Stir dry ingredients into the butter mixture. Beat into this the eggs and water. Cover and let stand about 2 hours or refrigerate overnight (this is important). Drop by tablespoonfuls on greased cookie sheet. Bake at 325° to 350° for 10 to 12 minutes. This makes 10 dozen cookies. They keep well. (Did I mention that they're good with milk?)

Makes 10 dozen.

Forgotten Cookies, *Catherine Kraft, Saranac Lake*

These cookies "bake" overnight in a pre-heated oven that has been turned off. They are my daughter's favorite Christmas cookies.

2 egg whites

²/₃ cup sugar

1 tsp. vanilla

1 cup chocolate chips

1 cup finely chopped walnuts

Beat egg whites until very stiff; gradually add the sugar. Fold in the other ingredients. Drop by teaspoonfuls on parchment paper (or plain brown paper like a grocery bag) placed on a cookie sheet. This recipe makes 2 cookie sheets of cookies. Keep the cookies fairly small so they get cooked all the way through. Place cookie sheets in pre-heated 325° oven. Turn oven off and leave overnight or at least 4 hours. (Put a sticky note on the oven so no one opens it or turns it on.)

Makes 2 dozen.

Bourbon Nut Cake, *Mary Valley, Wilmington*

I was visiting with my Florida friend Harriet on the telephone in early December as she was getting ready to send a special fruitcake to her son for Christmas. Harriet's late husband had come across the recipe in a newspaper many years earlier. Harriet worried the recipe would be lost when she was gone. I took the recipe and made it for my sister in Parishville, my father in Massena and for the Crested Hens. Everyone has found it to be delicious. This fruitcake will be eaten—do not expect to re-gift it from year to year.

4 cups flour

1 tsp. baking powder

4 tsp. nutmeg

1 cup butter

2 cups sugar

6 eggs

1 cup bourbon, divided

4 cups chopped pecans

1 lb. raisins

¹/₂ lb. candied cherries, chopped

Whisk together dry ingredients and set aside. In a separate bowl, cream butter and sugar. Add eggs one at a time alternately with ¹/₂ cup of bourbon. Add dry ingredients to egg mixture. Add pecans, raisins and cherries.

Bake in a Bundt pan at 300° for 2 hours. Cover with foil at the end of the baking time to prevent overbrowning. Cool and invert onto a cake plate. Before slicing, drizzle ¹/₂ cup of bourbon over cake. Slice when cool and sprinkle with confectioner's sugar. Or, instead of using straight bourbon as a drizzle, make a glaze of equal parts bourbon and confectioner's sugar.

(Note: when candied cherries cannot be found, you may use maraschino cherries.)

Right: *Holiday cookie decorations, Lake Placid Lodge.* Nancie Battaglia

Learning to Appreciate "Slow Food," *Chris Robinson, Hannawa Falls*

There were no food traditions in my family. Ours was an Irish Catholic household. This meant fish on Fridays and family meals on the holidays, but there were no special recipes passed down through the generations or unique rituals beyond saying grace. We were also an American family living through the '60s and '70s, an era of great advances in fast, processed foods.

A meal was time for us to gather around the table together, but it was a speedy affair. Food was fuel that staved off hunger pains and gave us the energy to get through the day. A particular line of processed foods cooked in "boiling bags," I recall, were very popular fare. From one pot of steaming water, a meal of Salisbury steaks, corn in butter sauce, and macaroni and cheese could be produced.

This was my gustatory inheritance. Through college and graduate school and into the start of professional life, food was a necessity requiring very little thought. I actually liked cafeteria food. Fast food first shaped and then fit this ethos. The first crack in this tradition occurred when I met my wife. Sunhee is Korean, a nation with food traditions as strong as the hot sauce that finds its way into every dish. It was clear from the beginning that the success of our relationship hinged on my ability to adapt to her dietary habits. That is, I had to begin to consider food seriously. We are still together.

With our move to the North Country we fell in

with a wonderful group of people who responded to the long winters by making meals the focus of social life. Food and wine shared around a long table invited laughter, conversation and ever-deepening friendship. I can mention meals I enjoy most—Hugo's paella and bouillabaisse, Maria's homemade chocolate ice cream and flans, Sunhee's vegetable pancakes—but my underdeveloped palate leaves me with a wider sense of what makes a good meal. It is the unrushed tempo of an evening with friends, the sensation of being in the warmth protected from the cold wind and snow outside, and the awakening that comes with new flavors and smells. To me, this pace and intimacy is the great gift of North Country cuisine. No doubt there is truth in the old saw, "You are what you eat," but the pace of eating and the company you keep are of equal importance.

Sunhee's Boochoo Juhn, *Sunhee and Chris Robinson, Hannawa Falls*

(Chris says: This was the first food Sunhee ever made for me. I was smitten on both counts.)

Start by washing and cutting leeks, zucchini and red peppers into thin slices about 1-inch in length.

You make the batter with flour and a special mix available in Asian food stores called buchim. There are also products that already combine the flour and buchim. You can also add an egg to the batter, but this is not necessary. The water to flour/buchim mix ratio is about 5 cups to 2. It is a relatively thick batter. Then add the cut vegetables to the batter.

Again, the mixture is thick. Add a little sesame oil to a frying pan (we use a non-stick pan). Then ladle some of the batter into the pan and smooth it. It will not spread like a traditional pancake; it needs a little help. Cook one side for about 3, maybe 4, minutes. Flip it when it is golden brown. Cook the other side.

The first side you cooked will always look the best. Serve it with that side up, and with a small dish of soy sauce on the side for dipping.

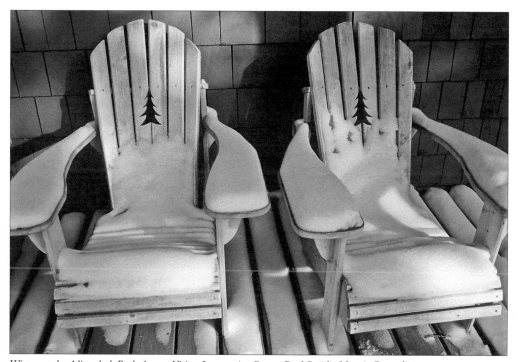

Winter at the Adirondack Park Agency Visitor Interpretive Center, Paul Smiths. Nancie Battaglia

Hanukkah, Shabbat or Any-Day-of-the-Year Challah, *Ellen Rocco, DeKalb*

This is wonderful for holidays and it makes great French toast when it starts to go stale. In the years when I had a Jersey cow and gallons of surplus milk and homemade butter, I made this bread with both of those ingredients. In truth, traditional Sabbath challah is probably closer to the recipe I offer below, precisely because it has no milk or butter and therefore may be served with meat meals in a kosher household.

4 1/2 cups warm water

3 packages or 3 generous tbsp. dry yeast

1/2 cup sugar

4 tsp. salt (generous well-rounded spoons)

1/3 cup vegetable oil (do not use olive oil)

10 eggs

4 to 5 lbs. white flour (you may use some whole wheat, but it won't have quite the same traditional consistency)

2 tbsp. poppy seeds

Dissolve yeast in warm water. Stir in sugar. After a couple of minutes, stir in salt and oil. In a separate smaller bowl, lightly beat 8 of the eggs, just to mix up eggs and whites. Add to water mixture. Stir in as much flour as necessary (it varies a lot based on moisture content of the flour you're using) to make a smooth, soft dough. Do not stir in so much flour that dough becomes stiff. Turn onto a floured board and knead for a couple of minutes. Grease the large bowl and return dough to it, flipping dough to leave oiled side up. Cover with a towel and let rise, about an hour. Dough should be about half again as big.

Turn dough onto a floured board, knead briefly (a minute or 2). Again, do not add a lot of flour. Dough should not stick, but it should not be really stiff.

Divide into 4 pieces. For each piece, to shape a loaf, do this: divide into thirds (or more pieces if you prefer to make a braid with 4 or 5 strands). Roll each piece between your palms to form a long tube of dough. Cross in middle and braid toward either end (or any other way you like to braid). Pinch ends of tubes together. Repeat for each loaf.

Place loaves on an oiled cookie sheet (you'll easily be able to fit 2 loaves on each sheet). Beat remaining 2 eggs with a couple of drops of water and brush tops and sides of each loaf, coating completely. Now sprinkle with poppy seeds.

Let rise for 30 to 45 minutes, then bake in 340° oven. Check position of bread at least once during baking—switch sheet on lower shelf to upper, rotate sheets from front to back. The object is to evenly cook through these very large loaves. It will take about 30 to 45 minutes. Loaves should be deeply brown and bottoms should be very firm.

Remove from sheets and cool on racks.

Makes 4 large loaves (freezes well).

Oscar's Adirondack Smoke House, Warrensburg. Nancie Battaglia

Saving Grace, *Dale Hobson, Potsdam*

It would have been 1958 or '59 on the early December day my father brought home his latest bargain. The backseat of the two-tone Buick contained 50 pounds of grain and 20 pounds of extremely tweaked live turkey. His theory was to use the one to feed the other up to a dignified corpulence appropriate to the guest of honor at Christmas dinner. Tom Turkey occupied a box in one corner of the cellar, while Ginger nursed her pups in the opposite corner next to the coal furnace, and we kids took turns trooping up and down the rickety stairs to keep everybody fed and watered. On Christmas Eve morning Dad took Tom away and came back with something large, plucked and headless for Mom to stuff. But I've always suspected that, in the end, he made a secret run to the A&P, after releasing Tom into some hedgerow out of town, where his descendants dodge traffic to this day. A bargain at twice the price.

Essex Farm Note, *Kristin and Mark Kimball, Essex*

Week 2, 2007

It's not that winter food is dull. The carrots will never be sweeter than they are right now, the kale is still coming in from the field, and from the root cellar come endless delicious combinations of celery root, beets, cabbage, leeks and rutabaga. (Delicious rutabaga? OK, that's a lie.) And without any fieldwork, we have time to fuss a little, experiment with a farmhouse cheese, or flip through the charcuterie recipes and seriously consider what it would take to make hot dogs from scratch. Still, there is a sameness to winter food.

Parsnips at a North Country vegetable stand. Nancie Battaglia

During the growing season, every week brings something new and inspiring into the kitchen. The first sweet spring peas beg to be cooked gently in milk and a little butter, North Country style, and served with a sprig of mint. And as soon as you're sated with peas, the first spinach comes in, and then the nasturtiums flower, adding their spicy note, and on and on through the end of fall. By midwinter, though, it's a matter of subtraction, not addition, and sometimes, facing what to make for supper, it feels like a long wait until pea season. That is when you know it's time to raid the shelves in the cellar and sort through the bags in the freezer, searching for a taste from summer. Last weekend I broke open a jar of pears that I canned back in August. I canned them on a hot Sunday, and the job got sticky and tedious, and I remember wondering if it was even worth it for the few quarts I'd get out of my half bushel. Last weekend I ate one of those quarts all by myself with the same gleeful, guilty abandon I've felt when ordering a second martini. The liquor from the jar smelled like pear blossoms. It was enough to make me laugh out loud. I ask you, when is the last time supermarket food made you laugh out loud? With *delight*? My pears *were* better than canned ones from the store with their tang of tin, but that's not all of it. The curse of the supermarket is that it offers instant gratification, seasons and geography be damned. Eating from the farm almost never offers instant gratification, but what it does offer is much better: satisfaction.

Calf at Clover Mead Farm, Keeseville. Nancie Battaglia

We brought a new cow home on New Year's Day. Emily. She is Mark's sister's cow, four years old, big boned for a Jersey. Linda Brook has been milking her for the better part of a year, but she and her husband have a three-year-old and a baby, and this winter the milking chores just got too laborious. It's been a pleasure to have some extra milk to play with, and Emily is a sweet and friendly cow. It took her about a minute to explain to the rest of the herd that, though new, she was not to be pushed around. Her only fault is her udder. Every teat is a different puzzle. But then, no cow is perfect. When our Melissa lets down, it's like turning on a milk faucet, but if she doesn't like the way you touch her udder, she'll kick, aiming for the full bucket or, if she's in a bad mood, your head.

The seed catalogs are open on the dining room table, big glossy pictures of fat, ripe tomatoes, copy that makes your mouth water. Once again I must be restrained from just ordering a packet of everything. This time of year is dangerous for me, because it's all fantasy, and no actual work.

That's the news for this satisfying second week of 2007. Find us at 518-963-4613, *kimball7@localnet.com*, or on the farm, any day but Sunday.

Handsome, Shelburne Farms, Shelburne VT. Nancie Battaglia

Spring

Regardless of the calendar, the North Country winter seems to last more than half the year. Just as the spirit develops an overwhelming hunger for that first promise of light and heat, an end to snow and the coming of green, so the appetite keens for more than what was put by, the dull winter trudge of starch and root crop, the desiccated provender of the freezer, and the tasteless facsimiles of produce jetted halfway round the world.

So we pounce upon the first fruits of the field with the lust of scurvied sailors reaching at last a tropic isle. Tender greens, fiddleheads, morels, asparagus, ramps—anything fresh and light—trout and lamb, milk that tastes of the pasture instead of the barn, the subtle creaminess of young cheese. Even though it comes every year, eventually, spring still tastes like hallelujah sounds.

Each week the weather gets better, and the palette for the palate grows richer, as garden and field fill in. Pungent rhubarb, the dreamy sweet-sour of strawberry, the crunch of snow pea and radish, the complex and smoky confection boiled down in sugarhouses. Spring in the stomach and spring in the step. Hallelujah. —**Dale Hobson**

Left: *Boiling sap, Lewis.* Nancie Battaglia

Spring Haiku, *Todd Moe, Norwood*

Cooped up for winter,
six plump hens now bathe in dirt.
We call it "the spa."

Wild Leeks, *Robin Rhodes-Crowell, Pierrepont*

Wild leeks are pungent beauties that can be added to everything from salad to stir-fry. The arrival of leeks—and other wild greens like nettles, cowslip and dandelion—means spring has arrived and the amount of available fresh local food will crescendo from now until September.

A wild leek (*Allium tricoccum*) is a scallion-like plant in the onion family with soft green broad leaves. The lower part of the stem is purple, leading underground to the white bulb. Wild leeks are almost always found in dense colonies in small moist valleys, growing well in deciduous forests from Canada to South Carolina. On a spring walk in the woods, leek tops may be the only green you can see from a distance. You may also spot trout lilies, spring beauties and trilliums growing near leek colonies. You'll need a spade or trowel to dig the leeks, so you can wiggle the bulbs free with one hand without breaking the leaves off. You'll smell the strong earthy garlic aroma of the leeks as you dig.

At the Indian Lake school, students and staff are involved in the school garden. Here, Ms. Schisler, a teaching assistant, explains seedlings in a window-box display made by reading teacher Ms. Currier. George DeChant, Indian Lake Central School, Indian Lake

I store leeks in an airtight container in the refrigerator and wash them as I use them. Once the thin outer skin is removed, the entire plant—leaves and bulb—may be used. Wild leeks are high in vitamins A and C, lutein and calcium. Early pioneers and Native Americans used wild leeks for both culinary and medicinal (spring tonic, antiseptic) purposes.

NCPR morning host Todd Moe and news director Martha Foley sample chef George Arnold's all-local spring omelet: eggs, wild morels and chives, soft goat cheese and asparagus, served with potatoes sautéed with ramps. NCPR web manager Dale Hobson, Canton

Left: *Friends, Shelburne Farms, Shelburne VT.* Nancie Battaglia.

Robin shared these two recipes with us:

Wild Leek Quiche (adapted from wild-leeks.com)

1 pie shell

¾ cup shredded cheddar cheese

1 tbsp. butter or oil

10 wild leeks, bulbs and leaves chopped or sliced

1 cup other vegetables, chopped (e.g., mushrooms, broccoli)

8 eggs

½ cup milk

1 tsp. crushed rosemary

1 tsp. crushed dill or oregano

Salt and pepper, to taste

Paprika or powdered red pepper

Preheat oven to 400°. Press pie dough into a pie plate or small casserole dish. Sprinkle ½ cup of cheese into pie shell. Sauté the leeks and other vegetables in a buttered or oiled pan until softened. Spread vegetables on top of cheese. In a large bowl, whisk together eggs, milk and seasonings. Pour over vegetables. Sprinkle top of quiche with paprika or red pepper. Bake for an hour, or until egg mixture has set and lightly browned.

Serves 6 to 8.

Wild Leek Casserole (adapted from main.nc.us)

1 tbsp. butter or oil

½ lb. sausage (pork, bison or venison)

5 eggs

2 cups grated cheese (cheddar or other favorite)

2 cups milk

Salt, pepper, thyme, rosemary or other seasonings, to taste

20 wild leeks, bulbs and tops sliced

8 small potatoes, sliced

Preheat oven to 350°. Brown the meat in the butter or oil. In a bowl, combine eggs, cheese, milk and seasonings. In a casserole dish, layer sausage, potatoes and wild leeks. Pour milk mixture over the top, sprinkle with a bit of grated cheese. Bake for approximately 1 hour, or until potatoes are tender.

Serves 4 to 5.

The Crested Hens celebrate Julie Robards' 50th with a Hen Party picnic somewhere in the High Peaks. Julie Robards

Chicken and Ramps (Wild Leeks), *Martha Clare Pritchard Spear, Upper Jay*

As soon as the weather indicates that spring is on the way, my brother and I start to make plans for our annual Mother's Day Ramps and Fiddlehead Fern Forage. It's a pilgrimage for me—a once-a-year chance to revisit my childhood. We take what seems like a dozen back roads to a very well-hidden spot next to a small stream where the banks are solid with the tulip-like leaves of the ramps. I was sworn to secrecy the first time my brother, who discovered the ramps years ago while trout fishing, took me with him. Digging ramps is messy—they must be coaxed gently but firmly from the ground. Back in my mother's kitchen, we are elbow deep in mud. Cleaning ramps is nearly as messy as digging them, but the kitchen fills with a rich earthy smell of onions and garlic—and spring. It is my brother's job to make a potato soup—a standard vichysoisse with ramps replacing cultivated leeks. My job is to roast the chicken.

1 lb. ramps

3 lbs. (more or less) chicken, cut up

1 lb. new potatoes

2 to 3 tbsp. quality olive oil

½ cup dry wine—good enough to drink!

1 cup chicken broth

Salt and pepper

Cut off and reserve the leaves from the ramps. Remove the roots and outer skin of the ramps but retain the slender pink stem on the bulbs. Place in separate bowls and set aside.

Rinse and pat dry chicken and potatoes and place in shallow roasting pan that can also go on top of the stove. Coat with 2 tbsp. of olive oil. Make sure chicken is skin side up. Season with salt and pepper and roast in 500° oven for 20 minutes.

While the chicken is cooking, mix ½ tbsp. oil with the ramp bulbs and season with salt. Add to chicken and potatoes and roast another 10 to 15 minutes or until chicken is cooked through. Remove chicken and roast veggies an additional 5 minutes or so, until tender. Remove ramps and potatoes and pour off fat.

Set the roasting pan on the top of the stove and deglaze with the wine over high heat. Reduce wine by half and add chicken broth. When it comes to a boil, quickly add the ramp leaves and cook only until wilted. Remove and add to platter with chicken and ramps and potatoes. Further reduce the broth, adjust the seasoning, pour around the platter and serve.

Serves 4.

The Elegance of Fiddleheads, *Robin Rhodes-Crowell, Pierrepont*

Foraging for wild foods was not on my list of Sunday activities while growing up in the suburbs of Cincinnati. For my husband, who grew up in the North Country, it is a natural rite of spring. Fiddleheads, with a simple, elegant flavor, are one of our seasonal favorites. Fiddleheads are the newly emerged coiled leaves of the ostrich fern.

Fiddleheads, Blue Mountain Lake. Nancie Battaglia

If you know what mature ostrich ferns look like (check a guidebook), you'll know where to look in early spring for the tightly wrapped fiddleheads soon after they appear above ground. Once they start to unfold, their time has passed. Look for fiddleheads in damp shady spots, either in woods or along hedgerows, usually growing in clumps. (Don't take too much from one spot, drift through your patch and pick from various spots.) When you get them to the kitchen, wash and rub off the brown, papery membrane. Fresh is best, so use them soon after harvesting. They go well with cheeses, such as Asiago and Parmesan, or may be steamed and eaten with a little butter and salt and pepper. Steamed fiddleheads may be chilled and added to salads or used with dips.

Note from Chef George: A friend may share a recipe with you, but a *true* friend will share the location of their favorite fiddlehead patch. (Make sure if you forage off of your own property that you have permission from the landowner.) Fiddleheads and ramps are among the edible wild foods found throughout the North Country that are available in the spring. Fiddlehead ferns appear as tightly furled fronds of the plant *Matteuccia struthiopteris*; the plant's name comes from its resemblance to the scroll on a violin. I like to steam mine and serve them with a sauce of sautéed shallots, fresh lemon juice, warmed mayonnaise and black pepper.

Vermont Fiddlehead Pie, *The Combes Family Inn, Ludlow VT*

1 uncooked 9-inch pie crust

2 cups fiddleheads, coarsely chopped

1 small chopped onion

2 tbsp. olive oil

1 cup shredded cheddar cheese

4 eggs

1 cup milk or half-and-half

1 tbsp. coarse mustard

2 tbsp. flour

Salt, pepper or other light
seasonings, to taste

Preheat oven to 350°. Precook pie crust in oven. Sauté fiddleheads and onion in olive oil. Spread in pie crust, followed by cheese. In a bowl, blend remaining ingredients, then pour over pie. Bake for 50 minutes or until a knife comes out clean when inserted into pie. Let set for 5 minutes, then cut. Serve hot, warm or cold, as you would quiche.

Note from Chef George: One of the delights of spring is the return of fresh greens. New greens with a fresh-tasting dressing delight our palates and refresh our taste buds. I like the use of maple syrup as a sweetener in the following recipe. When making a dressing always remember the old adage: be a spendthrift with the oil and a miser with the vinegar—typically 4 or 5 parts oil to 1 part vinegar.

Lemon Maple Vinaigrette, *Amy Fennelly, Upper Jay*

This has just the right balance of tart and sweet and is delicious on young greens.

¹/₂ cup olive oil or canola oil

2 tbsp. wine or rice wine vinegar

3 tbsp. fresh lemon juice

1 tbsp. maple syrup or honey

¹/₂ scant tsp. salt

1 tsp. Dijon mustard

Dried thyme, basil and black pepper,
to taste

Mix it all up in a bottle and keep refrigerated.

Spring is a season of holidays—if nothing else, the break in the weather calls for celebration. Here are a few samples of traditional foods brought to the North Country from other cultures, other places.

Peta de Spinoche (Spinach Pie), *Jackie Sauter, Canton*

When the Sephardic Jews fled Spain in 1492 they took their food traditions with them to their new homes in the Ottoman Empire (primarily what is now Turkey and Greece) and incorporated local produce and food techniques—lemons, garlic, olives, almonds, rosewater, spinach, herbs, filo—into their cuisine. Here's an easy Americanized version of an old recipe that my grandmother Esther DeMayo got from her grandmother who probably got it from her grandmother. It's nice when made with fresh spinach in the spring.

A few tbsp. olive oil

1 onion, chopped

1 to 2 cloves of garlic, chopped

10 to 15 oz. fresh spinach, chopped

1/2 tsp. oregano

Salt and pepper, to taste

1 tsp. lemon juice

4 cups cottage cheese or farmers' cheese (can use feta for 1/4 of the cheese)

4 eggs, beaten

Sauté chopped onion in oil until just transparent. Add chopped garlic and sauté a few minutes more. Add chopped spinach, oregano, salt and pepper, and lemon juice. Sauté just until ingredients are thoroughly mixed and heated through. Remove from heat.

In a bowl, mix beaten eggs and cheese. Add spinach and stir to mix. Traditionally, the filling was poured over a crust made of moistened matzohs, but it's equally wonderful in a filo dough crust, a regular pie crust or just poured into a greased casserole and baked. You can top it with crust or filo, or just sprinkle the top with coarsely chopped matzoh, walnuts, pecans or almonds. Bake in a 400° oven for approximately 1 hour. Cooking time will vary depending on crust and size of dish. It's done when the spinach is soft and the filling has set.

Serves 6 to 8.

Passover Haiku, *Bonnie in Florida via Ellen Rocco, DeKalb*

On Passover we
opened the door for Elijah.
Now our cat is gone.

Right: *Around the Passover Seder table, DeKalb.* Laura Von Rosk, Schroon Lake

Russian Easter, *Sonia Dowgiallo, Minerva*

These are traditional Russian recipes that were brought to this country by my husband Mike's father, Alexander Alexandrovitch Emelianoff, and by my mother, Katerina Hemke Dowgiallo. It is an age-old Russian tradition to prepare these dishes for Easter. The recipes make more than one family would eat, as it is the custom to share this food with friends and neighbors, and sample theirs as well. These dishes are very rich and sweet with all the ingredients one isn't supposed to eat during Lent.

Mike and I have carried on the tradition (I do the baking), using recipes from both sides of our families, and we continue the tradition of passing these delicious dishes on to family, friends and neighbors.

Spring North Country lambs. Nancie Battaglia

Alexander Emelianoff's Paska

*P*aska, made with heavy cream, eggs and goat cheese or farmers' cheese, is poured into a hand-carved wooden mold lined with cheese cloth, then pressed with weights for 1 to 2 days to drain and firm to proper consistency. This recipe was brought to this country by Alexander in the 1930s, and presented to Mike's mom in the '40s. The original recipe was in measurements of "a pinch of this and a dash of that." Mike's mom, Beatrice, spent the next 60 years refining it into the recipe here.

2 lbs. farmers' cheese

$\frac{1}{2}$ lb. sweet butter

12 pt. sweet cream

2 cups sugar (fine-blend in processor with vanilla)

1 stick vanilla bean

$\frac{1}{2}$ to 1 cup blanched, finely chopped almonds

$\frac{1}{2}$ lb. dried fruit (currants, pineapple, etc.)

Blend in processor one at a time.

Drain in cheesecloth and mold with weights overnight.

Katerina Dowgiallo's Kulich

*K*ulich is a sweet bread made in large volume, put into 12 to 16 coffee cans because there is so much, and then baked. This recipe is my mom's.

8 eggs

3 cups sugar or 1 $\frac{1}{2}$ cups honey, plus 1 extra tbsp. sugar

2 vanilla beans or 2 tbsp. vanilla

4 packages yeast

1 cup warm water

2 24-oz. cans evaporated milk, skimmed

5 lbs. flour, approximately

4 sticks sweet butter, very soft

Grated lemon rind

1 to 2 cups finely chopped, blanched almonds

3 cups raisins, soaked in hot water to soften

Beat eggs 3 minutes, then add sugar or honey and vanilla beans or vanilla. Add yeast dissolved in warm water with a tbsp. of sugar and evaporated milk. Add flour (a little at a time), sweet butter (alternate flour with butter), grated lemon rind, almonds and raisins. Knead 20 to 30 minutes. Let it rise, punch down. Separate into greased and breadcrumb-coated coffee can tin. Let it rise again, about 45 minutes. Bake in preheated 325° oven for about 40 minutes.

A pre-Easter conference between Marshmallow and Sean; eggs are their natural colors, provided by Araucana hens. Marilyn Mayer, Canton

Hare Today, Gone Tomorrow, *Elizabeth Folwell, Blue Mountain Lake*

In the 1980s the Adirondack Lakes Center for the Arts, in Blue Mountain Lake, used to put on an amazing community feast. We're not talking about pancakes and sausage or strawberry shortcake but a full-blown seven-course meal for 150 people, in the depths of mud season. This sounds daunting enough, but the reality—turning the arts center, a former garage, into a restaurant with multiple stoves and refrigerators plus candlelit tables and a stage for a dance band—was akin to making a silk steamer trunk from a sow's ear.

An array of gas ranges from summer places came by truck, unneeded in their usual kitchens. Same with freezers and fridges, even a huge sink for prep and clean up. The arts center's pottery studio looked pretty close to a commercial kitchen within a day, and various talented local cooks washed, pared, trimmed and chopped all the ingredients for courses that included crab bisque, shrimp scampi, homemade sorbet, salad of marinated cauliflower and black olives, and tiramisu. Steaks were grilled outside, sometimes the seafood course too, and an army of volunteers performed like a seasoned restaurant crew.

The clientele for this Brigadoon of eateries was friends and neighbors. Each course came with the appropriate wine, the right music. At the end of one dinner, a lady who hunted, trapped, collected berries and made fabulous apple pies, told me, "I never stuck a fork into a more elegant meal in my life." It is hard now to imagine the words "elegant" and "downtown Blue Mountain Lake" in the same conversation, but there you have it—a testimonial for the ages.

That evening my neighbor and I continued talking about food, what we like, what we don't, and I admitted that while I love venison I had never tasted rabbit. Our chat took a few other turns, and the night proceeded into the wee hours, as dishes were trucked into yet another kitchen for washing and packing into their rental boxes.

The next day we were still cleaning up. When I returned home, there were two beautiful snowshoe hares ready for the Dutch oven on my doorstep. I was astonished and pleased, but also at a loss for just how to prepare them with the care and respect they deserved. They were a gift from an elderly woman who had stewed muskrats, pickled deer hearts, fried bullheads, made chokecherry jam and had the turn of the seasons dictate what went on the table. In sap season, as the snowshoe hares begin changing color, they become more visible against fresh snow. They are part of an Adirondack early spring, just like maple syrup.

When I called to thank her I also asked for cooking tips. Her advice was simple, to quarter the rabbits, dredge them in flour with a little salt and pepper and fry the pieces in lard (sorry, we used butter) until golden. Then she suggested adding some sliced apples and onions to the pan, sautéing them until the fragrance filled the room. Then, a little cider vinegar, a little brown sugar, a little scraping to be sure nothing was sticking and put the rabbit back in, covering the skillet. After an hour, the meat would fall off the bones. On the side, she said, egg noodles with lots of butter.

People who say rabbit tastes like chicken have never had country pullets or wild snowshoe hares. The flavor was pared down to the essence of a wild meat that reflects the woods on which it depends. The texture shows the life the animal led, young and tender or experienced and sinewy. But pushing back from the table that night, I felt that I too had just put my fork into something elegant, connected to our world and the people who call it home.

Maple Diner, Old Forge. Nancie Battaglia

The "Morel" of the Story, *Todd Moe, Norwood*

Growing up in rural Minnesota, spring was always my favorite season. Too early for haying or weeding the garden, it was a time for exploring the woods, building tree forts and getting my sneakers soaked scouring the swamp for frogs.

I grew up in a family with an interest in gardening, but not wild edibles, and there was nothing New Age about my parents. But I remember when my dad found a patch of morel mushrooms behind the barn. He'd gone out before lunch, on a whim (or childhood memory), and came back with his cap full of conical "shrooms" with the distinctive honeycomb pattern. Mom and I skeptically watched as Dad sliced the morels and fried them in butter for a few minutes. "You first!" we chimed as he spooned the wrinkled, brown samples onto a dinner plate. Dad beamed as he speared one with his fork. I realized after his third or fourth mouthful that he knew his edible fungus. For me, it was love at first bite, and the start of years of hunting the elusive morel. Memorial Day became *Memorel* Day as a way of remembering this annual euphoric ritual.

It's hard to describe what a morel mushroom tastes like. Author Larry Lonik surveyed morel hunters for his book, *The Curious Morel: Mushroom Hunters' Recipes, Lore and Advice.* Responses varied from, "thinly sliced sirloin steak," "steamed clams," "chewy," "delicate" and "after a day in the woods, like gold." Its aroma is primal, like something from an ancient forest. It's equally hard to explain their lure. Why go after something that most people recoil from? Maybe that's it. We're having *fungus* for dinner!

Morels are elusive. And there are many theories as to when, where and why they make their appearance. Since most fungi live on decaying material, you'll most likely find morels among dead and dying hardwoods like elm, ash or remnants of apple orchards. However, I came across my first North Country morels right in the middle of our back lawn in Norwood. But it's usually not that easy. They're experts at camouflage and they blend in with beds of leaves and among pine needles in the woods. I usually find them from early May through mid-June. Late spring rains and warm nights are a good sign.

There are morel hunting clubs, an annual Morel Mushroom Festival in Michigan and even (gasp!) a morel habitat kit to grow them in your backyard. But then, where's the joy of the hunt?

There's an old saying, "You can eat any mushroom once." So, take care. Edible morels are hollow. False morels (poisonous) are not hollow, which is the most definite tip that you've stumbled on a mycological "bad boy." All morels should be well cooked. I could make a meal of morels, but they're also great in omelettes, and with pasta or meat. Bumper crops can be dried on screens for a couple of weeks and stored in canning jars or plastic bags, or frozen, and added to winter soups. *Larousse Gastronomique* says, "Morels with dark caps ... sometimes called black morels ... are the most highly-prized ones. The paler variety is less tasty." But trust me—never turn down an edible morel!

So, what is the morel ... er, moral of this story? Hey, even though the idea of eating wild mushrooms seems eccentric or foolish to most people, these tasty little treasures are enough to tempt even the fungiphobic. And did I mention that the morel became Minnesota's official state fungus in 1984? Ya, you betcha!

Here's a quick and easy recipe:

Easy Chicken with Morels

6 to 8 fresh morels, washed and split in half

6 chicken breasts

1 tbsp. butter

Small chopped shallot or onion

2 tbsp. heavy cream

Salt, pepper and nutmeg

Dip chicken breasts in flour and brown on both sides in a pan with butter and shallot or onion. Season with salt and pepper and a pinch of nutmeg. Add morels, cover pan and cook for 7 to 8 minutes. Add heavy cream and cook another 10 to 15 minutes uncovered. Serve with potatoes or wild rice.

Serves 6.

NCPR morning host Todd Moe filled his hat with morel mushrooms during an early summer walk.
Todd Moe, Norwood

Saturday Opera Chicken Soup, *Christine Mace, Canton*

*O*ne of my earliest memories of North Country Public Radio was growing up with the Saturday afternoon opera broadcasts. I was introduced to Pavarotti, among other singers, when my mother, Phoebe Gauthier, would listen to the Met broadcasts, which meant we all listened. I learned to enjoy the music and because Mother often made chicken soup, from a recipe she learned from her mother, Catherine Catanzarite, during those broadcasts, I loop Saturday opera with homemade chicken soup—both delicious!

6 qts. water

1 chicken, whole or cut up

4 stalks of celery, cut on the slant in 1-inch pieces

6 large carrots, peeled and cut on the slant in 1-inch pieces

1 medium onion, cut in half

1 can whole tomatoes

1 tbsp. parsley, fresh chopped or dried

1 lb. acini de pepe or other tiny pasta

Put everything except the pasta into a large pot and bring to a boil. Then, turn down to simmer and cook for 2 hours. Cook pasta separately and mix into soup. Serve.

Sometimes when Grandma Catanzarite would make this soup she would roll tiny chicken meatballs and add to the soup. The Italian mother of a friend of mine also made this soup, and counted out precisely the same number of meatballs into each child's bowl so there was no squabbling about who had more. When I eat this soup, I think of my mother and grandmother, and of listening to opera on NCPR.

Serves 6 to 10.

Above: *The late John and Marie Fontana make cookies, Cold River Ranch, Tupper Lake.* Right: *Fly-fishing the Ausable River.* Nancie Battaglia (2)

Trout Haiku, *Michael Coffey, New York City*

Trout stream high and cold.
Where the hell are my waders?
On second thought, nah.

Sole from Larry the Fish Guy, *Paul Graham, Canton*

I must celebrate Larry the Fish Guy because he is a North Country staple and because I love him dearly. Every Thursday, April through December, he appears outside the Canton post office to sell fish from the back of his truck. There is a faded lobster (I think it's grinning) painted on the side. I have never known Larry to cancel on us, but if you miss Larry in Canton, you can catch him in Potsdam or Sackets Harbor or Alexandria Bay. He moves east to west, emptying out his ice chests as he goes.

Larry the Fish Guy, Canton.
Nancie Battaglia

Growing up, I was told to never, ever buy fish from the roadside. "You want hepatitis?" my mother would say. "There it is. Bon appétit." But *au contraire*: I've had better fish out of the back of Larry's truck than I've had within view of the Atlantic. Larry has salmon, halibut, sole, tuna, haddock, rainbow trout, mahimahi and cod; live lobsters, a little disoriented, wrapped in damp newspaper; shrimp, scallops, clams and mussels. And occasionally he has crab-cake sandwiches.

Larry bends down to dig in the ice for your request and lifts it out with two hands, as if he had plunged them into the sea itself. Then he holds the filet or steak out over the gate for you to inspect the color, the thickness and even to take a sniff, if you would like.

Such food is often best treated simply, but sometimes it instills in me a mad desire to bang pots, chop, sizzle, flip, pour and stir. Hence this recipe, a reliable imitation of several recipes from several restaurants. It's pleasing on one of those nights in April or May when it is spring in most parts of the country but not here.

Sole with Shrimp and Herbed Cream Sauce

1 lb. fresh sole

³/₄ lb. fresh shrimp, raw, peeled and deveined

1 cup heavy cream

2 tbsp. unsalted butter

2 shallots, minced

1 cup minced red pepper

2 tbsp. fresh herbs (parsley, rosemary, thyme), or 2 tsp. Old Bay Seasoning

Salt and pepper, to taste

Preheat the oven to 350°. Melt butter in a heavy-bottomed pan, then sauté shallots in butter over medium heat for 2 minutes. Add red pepper and sauté 2 minutes more, then add shrimp. Continue cooking until shrimp begin to turn pink and curl, about 2 minutes. Add salt and pepper, to taste, and any herbs (a little tarragon works well, as does parsley, thyme or rosemary). Add cream and cook until just simmering, stirring constantly so the cream does not scald. Continue to cook until cream has slightly reduced and thickened into a pleasing sauce, about 5 minutes. Set aside.

Grease a medium-sized gratin or casserole dish. Lay out the sole filets on a cutting board, and salt and pepper both sides. Spoon a small amount of the shrimp mixture onto the thicker edge of filet, then roll. When you place the fish in the gratin dish, set the loose end on the bottom to hold in place. (If the loose ends refuse to settle, you can spear the roll with a toothpick, but be careful to remove them when serving.) Stuff and roll remaining filets, reserving a portion of the cream sauce to pour over the top when finished. Cover and bake for 15 to 20 minutes.

Serves 2 to 3.

Weekly lineup for fresh seafood at Larry the Fish Guy's truck, Canton.
Nancie Battaglia

Shrimp Robardini, *Terry Robards, Upper Jay*

*T*erry has prepared this dish for company hundreds of times over the course of 25 years. Most recently he demonstrated the cooking of it to an ambitious young chef who came for dinner who confessed after the meal that he didn't like lima beans but having them prepared this way had changed his mind. We sometimes serve it with spinach linguini nests and a cold, crisp Sauvignon Blanc. It is out of this world!

1 box frozen Fordhook lima beans

1 ¹/₂ lbs. extra large shrimp, peeled, cleaned and deveined

3 cloves garlic, minced

5 tbsp. good quality extra virgin olive oil

Fleur de sel sea salt

Begin by cooking Fordhook lima beans according to package directions in salted, boiling water.

While limas are cooking, heat a large nonstick frying pan over medium heat. Add approximately 3 tbsp. olive oil and sauté minced garlic for about 3 minutes. Avoid browning—cook garlic until it is slightly translucent. Add another tbsp. of oil to coat entire surface of pan and add shrimp in a single layer over garlic. Do not stir. Raise heat to medium high and let shrimp cook for approximately 3 to 4 minutes, until underside is bright pink but top surface is still gray. Remove pan from heat and turn shrimp individually with tongs. Return to heat and cook another 3 to 4 minutes, until shrimp are pink and thoroughly cooked but not overcooked.

While shrimp finish cooking, heat an ovenproof serving bowl in oven or microwave. Drain beans. Transfer hot shrimp and garlic to heated serving bowl and add drained beans. Toss gently and drizzle with remaining olive oil. Season with fleur de sel.

Serves 4.

Clam Chowder, *Ken Hall, DeKalb*

*A*bout 25 years ago I was working with the FB-111 flight simulator group at Plattsburgh Air Force Base. I occasionally went to Pease, our sister base in New Hampshire. One day at lunch a captain said, "I am going to take you to a place that serves the best clam chowder you have ever eaten." I was not a fan of canned clam chowder, so it was with a bit of trepidation that I accompanied him. But it was excellent. After much experimenting, I came up with what must be close to that recipe.

14 oz. can chopped clams (or fresh chopped clams if available)

4 oz. bacon

1 lb. potatoes, diced into 3/4-inch cubes

3/4 lb. onions, chopped

2 cups half-and-half

In a heavy pot brown the bacon. Add onions into cooked bacon and cook until onion is translucent. Drain the grease. Open clams and pour with juice into pot with bacon and onion. Place potatoes into pot with bacon, clams, onion and juice. The juice will just cover the potatoes. If not, add enough clam juice or water to do so (clam juice preferred). Stir and bring mixture to a boil and simmer until potatoes are cooked.

Pour the half-and-half into the mixture and continue to cook until the half-and-half is heated.

Serve with dense bread and butter, or not, and cold beer. Do not add salt (bacon has plenty), but add pepper, to taste (pre-ground acceptable).

Soup consistency is thin. Do not add flour or cornstarch to soup to thicken.

Serves 6.

Note from Chef George: Ken's original recipe could have fed all of the pilots at the Air Force Base. We've reduced it to family size.

Robert has spent the last few summers as Ellen Rocco's houseguest. He is a New Orleans native who has adopted the North Country as his second home. Robert became a dedicated summer volunteer at the Potsdam Food Co-op and always cooked an exotic Louisiana specialty at neighborhood potlucks. This is one of those recipes.

Creole Cream Crab Soup, *Robert Hoffman, DeKalb*

This bisque can be served at an elegant dinner party or as a splittin' wood soup. Either way, it's so simple to prepare that you'll feel like you're cheating. Cheating has never tasted so good.

1 bunch green onions, chopped

1 ½ sticks butter, melted

1 can white corn

4 cans cream of celery soup

2 cans creamed corn

1 qt. half-and-half

1 ½ lbs. crabmeat

3 capfuls of Zataran's Liquid Crab Boil (if necessary substitute Old Bay Seasoning or a generous pinch of thyme and a bit of bay leaf)

Salt and pepper

Sauté green onions in butter. Add white corn and continue to cook 2 to 3 minutes. Add the creamed corn and cream of celery soup and heat slowly. Add half-and-half, crabmeat and Zataran's and simmer. Season with salt and pepper, to taste.

Serve with a warm baguette from the Potsdam Food Co-op's bakery.

Serves 16.

In early spring goats gather on a sun-warmed rock, Hermon. Scott Sutherland, Hermon

---

Spring Growth Haiku, *Leon Le Beau, Colton*

Spring thinks about growth;
after such a long winter,
so does my waistband!

Making Gumbo in the North Country, *Anne Gregson, Schroon Lake*

I lived in Louisiana for six years during my early 20s and learned to make a pretty decent gumbo. It's hard tracking down okra in the North Country. Gotta have the okra. And filé, the thickening spice you add at the very end. On the 45-minute drive to Glens Falls, I first stop at Oscar's Adirondack Smoke House, in Warrensburg, for andouille sausage—a spicy one. You can substitute kielbasa but, as the song goes, "Ain't nothin' like the real thing, baby." In Glens Falls, I go to a store that has fresh okra and fresh fish. I buy raw shrimp, raw oysters and crabmeat in a can. Back home, it all goes together just fine and I'm ready to serve it up to my buds.

> **Note from Chef George:** According to Wikipedia, gumbo is a stew or soup originating in Louisiana, and found across the Gulf Coast and into the U.S. South. It consists primarily of a strong stock, meat and/or shellfish, a thickener and the vegetable "holy trinity" of celery, bell peppers and onion. The soup is traditionally served over rice.
>
> If you want to make a North County gumbo, you could skip the okra and substitute cornstarch blended with thyme, ground bay leaf and coriander for the filé powder and made into a slurry. Cut green beans can substitute for the texture and look of the okra, but, of course, will not provide the thickening, for which you will need to rely on the cornstarch.
>
> Please note that there are two thickeners in this stew: the roux, which also provides flavor (if done correctly), and the cornstarch, which will provide the silkiness (or "sliminess") the okra usually gives. It has been written that okra and filé in a gumbo is like wearing a belt and suspenders!
>
> Many gumbos are made without filé powder. In fact, the great Paul Prudhomme makes many of his gumbos with neither filé powder nor okra.

Food sign, Hopkinton. Nancie Battaglia

Sugar shack at Yancey's, a 150-year-old family-owned maple products business in Croghan. Nancie Battaglia

Foods of Spring

There are three foods I associate with North Country spring more than any others—not counting last year's softening onions or potatoes with eyes sprouting white shoots or once-youthful butternuts now wrinkling at their ends. They are: maple syrup, wild leeks (called ramps everywhere else but here) and rhubarb. Greens were covered earlier in this section, but stay tuned—you'll get the maple and rhubarb. —ER

Maple-Cranberry Barbecue Sauce, *George Arnold, Potsdam*

There are numerous "You know you live in northern New York when ..." jokes, but one humorous sight—although no joke—is the first barbecue of spring. More than once I've seen someone cooking outdoors while there is still snow on the ground wearing their wool cap with earflaps down to protect them from the cold. Yes, hope springs eternal, and it doesn't take much of a break in the weather for us to feel that spring is here or at least around the corner. In that spirit I present Cranberry-Maple Barbecue Sauce—a marriage of fall and spring ingredients.

2 tbsp. oil

1/2 cup onions, chopped

1 can cranberry sauce, whole berry

1/2 cup apple cider vinegar

1 cup maple syrup

1/2 cup ketchup

1 chili in adobo (optional)

Sauté onions in oil until translucent. Add all other ingredients and bring to a boil. Simmer 5 minutes. Remove from heat and puree in a blender or food processor. Thin with hot water as necessary.

Beef and Pork Marinade, *Sandy Demarest, Potsdam*

When a chef was asked by a finicky customer if his meat was easily chewed, the chef replied, "Of course it is, I serenaded it all night." Said the customer, "Oh yeah, what d'ya sing, 'Love Me Tender?'" Old joke. But this marinade will do the job, deliciously.

1 cup soy sauce

1 cup dry white wine or vermouth

1 bunch scallions, chopped

1 tbsp. North Country honey

3 cloves crushed garlic

Combine all ingredients. In an appropriate container, spread meat, pour marinade over meat, cover and refrigerate (for at least a few hours, overnight is better). While grilling or broiling, brush marinade over meat frequently.

Maple syrup grades, South Meadow Farm, Lake Placid. Nancie Battaglia

Getting Ourselves into a Real Rhubarb

Until I moved north, I'd never experienced rhubarb. I knew the word but had never tasted or seen the plant. These days, if you drive past my place in early spring, you'll find me out in the garden, planting peas or spinach and snacking on tender new rhubarb stalks—yes, raw. Most often, I simply cut the rhubarb up and cook it down with sugar, to taste, and perhaps a bit of cinnamon or similar seasoning. It can easily be canned (high acid) or frozen in this cooked-down state. But, like zucchini, when rhubarb comes in, there's just so much of it it's hard to use it all. So consider the following an act of public service: lots of ideas for using that miraculous rhubarb, the plant that comes back every year, provides pounds and pounds of food, and transforms itself into one of the most spectacular flowering plants in the yard when the peak harvesting season has passed. —ER

Riley Douglas shares wild blueberries at Balanced Rock, on the hike up Pitchoff Mountain near the Cascade Lakes. Nancie Battaglia

Note from Chef George: Around for years and still one of the best, I recommend this *American Classic Fannie Farmer* recipe for rhubarb sauce. Peel and cut rhubarb in 1-inch pieces. Put in a saucepan, sprinkle generously with sugar, and add enough water to prevent rhubarb from burning. Rhubarb contains such a large percentage of water that little additional water is needed. Cook until soft. If rhubarb is covered with boiling water, allowed to stand 5 minutes, then drained and cooked, less sugar will be required. Rhubarb is sometimes baked in an earthen pudding dish. If baked slowly for a long time it has a rich red color.

Red Currant Rhubarb Sauce with Port Wine, *George Arnold, Potsdam*

2 cups rhubarb, washed, peeled and diced in ¼-inch pieces (about 1 lb.)

1 ¼ cups red currant jelly

1 tbsp. arrowroot

½ oz. port wine

Combine the rhubarb with the red currant jelly and cook over medium heat until reduced by about ⅓. Strain the rhubarb out of the sauce. You should have about 1 cup of liquid. If you have more, reduce over medium heat until the desired 1 cup is reached. Save the cooked rhubarb and chill it overnight. This can be served just like you would applesauce with a pork chop. Combine the port wine and arrowroot and stir out any lumps. Add the port mixture to the boiling rhubarb sauce and stir vigorously. Simmer for 2 minutes to cook out the starch. Excellent with grilled meats or poultry.

Makes 12 servings.

Rhubarb Relish, *Penny LeBeau, Colton*

This recipe comes from my aunt who lived in Dalhousie, New Brunswick.

2 cups apple cider vinegar

4 cups brown sugar

1 tsp. salt

1 tsp. cinnamon

½ tsp. ground allspice

½ tsp. ground cloves

¼ tsp. black pepper

1 qt. rhubarb, cut into 1-inch pieces

1 qt. onions, chopped fine

Mix together the sugar, seasonings and vinegar. Add the onions and rhubarb. Boil gently until fairly thick. Pour into sterilized jars and seal.

Makes 32 servings.

Rhubarb Chutney, *Mary Hussmann, Canton*

I have a big rhubarb plant and found this recipe courtesy of Rachael Ray. She has her roots in the North Country, having grown up in Lake George. It's excellent with savory dishes like grilled pork chops. (See rachaelray.com for more recipes and ideas from this North Country native.)

2 tbsp. butter

3 tbsp. sugar

1 tbsp. lemon juice

¹/₄ cup balsamic vinegar

2 cups rhubarb, chopped

¹/₂ cup golden raisins

Melt butter in saucepan. Add sugar, lemon juice and vinegar and bring to a bubble. Add the rhubarb and raisins and simmer 8 to 10 minutes or until rhubarb is tender.

Makes 8 servings.

Helen Ordway Cornwall's Rhubarb Conserve, *Helen Ordway Cornwall, Johnsburg*

C ourtesy of From the Hearth and The Recipe Box, *collected for the Town of Johnsburg Bicentennial.*

4 qt. rhubarb, cut small

2 lbs. sugar

4 oranges, thinly sliced

2 lemons, thinly sliced

1 lb. raisins

¹/₂ lb. walnuts, coarsely chopped

Put all ingredients in large pot and cook, stirring well. Continue cooking and stirring until proper consistency. I test for desired consistency by chilling a little bit of the conserve in a sauce dish in the refrigerator. Control heat and stir often to keep from sticking to bottom. Be patient. Put in jars and process.

Above: *UShare volunteers David Bradford, Jan DeWaters, Jane Lavigne, Miles Manchester and Linda Camano plant broccoli and beans at the Cecilie Garden, in Potsdam; vegetables from the garden are donated to local food shelves during the harvest.* NCPR's Todd Moe, Norwood. Right: *Morning in the Adirondacks.* Nancie Battaglia

Rhubarb Haiku, *Todd Moe, Norwood*

Early riser. Red
rhubarb. Crisp in cool, spring soil.
Soon, there's talk of pie!

Rhubarb-Orange Pie, *Lynn Case Ekfelt, Canton*

I grew up in the suburbs of Buffalo amid manicured lawns with not a cow in sight. But every Sunday after church we'd ride out into the country to buy our eggs from Mrs. Miller. She and Mom would chat while I'd play with the big Lab, Blackie. In spring Mom always added rhubarb to her egg order. The season was never long enough for us to get our fill of rhubarb sauce, rhubarb shrub and rhubarb pie. Sometimes we had straightforward, two-crust pie, and sometimes when something a little fancier was called for, we had this one—a recipe from Mrs. Miller.

Pastry for a 9-inch, 1-crust pie

Filling:

3 egg whites

⅟₂ cup sugar

3 egg yolks

⅟₂ cup sugar

1 cup flour

1 cup butter, soft

3 tbsp. orange juice concentrate

1 tbsp. orange rind, grated

2 cups rhubarb, cut into ⅟₂-inch pieces

Line the pie pan with the pastry, making a fluted rim.

Beat the egg whites until stiff. Add ⅟₂ cup of the sugar by tbsp., beating well after each addition.

Mix the remaining ⅟₂ cup of sugar thoroughly with the flour. Add this to the egg yolks along with the butter, orange juice concentrate and orange rind. Beat well. Add the rhubarb, mixing thoroughly. Fold in the meringue.

Pour the mixture into the pastry shell. Bake at 375° for 15 minutes, then turn down the heat to 325° and bake for 45 minutes more.

Serves 6 to 8.

Inset painting: A Good Time Coming, *1863.* Arthur Tait

Here's the modern version: Fellows from Massachusetts, Vermont, western New York and the North Country preparing a camp feast at a lean-to site on the Raquette River upstream from Coreys, May 2006. John Littlefield, Boston MA

Rhubarb Crunch, *Laurie Smith, Canton*

Mix together:

4 cups rhubarb, cut into 1-inch pieces

³/₄ cup sugar

2 tbsp. flour

2 tbsp. melted butter

Pour into 8- or 9-inch baking dish.

Set oven for 375°.

Mix until crumbly:

³/₄ cup sugar (brown sugar is great)

1 cup flour

1 tsp. baking powder

¹/₂ to 1 tsp. salt

1 egg, beaten

¹/₄ cup oatmeal

Sprinkle over rhubarb mixture and shake pan. Bake for 30 to 40 minutes.

Serves 6.

Rhubarb Upside-Down Cake, *Evelyn Greene, North Creek*

3 tbsp. butter, melted

¹/₂ cup brown sugar

2 cups rhubarb, diced

¹/₄ cup dry sherry

3 egg yolks

1 tsp. lemon juice

¹/₂ cup sugar

¹/₄ cup hot water

1 cup flour

1 ¹/₂ tsp. baking powder

¹/₄ tsp. salt

3 egg whites

¹/₄ cup sugar

Mix melted butter with brown sugar and spread it over the bottom of a 9-inch baking dish. Spread chopped rhubarb over. Drizzle sherry over rhubarb. Next, beat the egg yolks with the lemon juice and sugar until thick but light. Slowly beat in the hot water. In another bowl, sift together the flour, baking powder and salt. Stir this into the yolk mixture. Next, beat the egg whites until they stiffen, adding the sugar slowly. Fold this into the flour-yolk mixture. Spread mixture over the rhubarb and bake in a 325° oven until done, about an hour.

Remove from oven, let stand 5 minutes, loosen sides, invert on plate. Serve warm with whipped cream.

Serves 6.

Helen's Rhubarb Custard Pie, *Jackie Sauter, Canton*

*C*risp, cobbler, crumble, buckle, grunt, slump. There are lots of great recipes for using rhubarb in the springtime, but we never get past this favorite, which comes from Radio Bob's mother. Rhubarb freezes well and easily. To keep the pies coming all year long, just chop a pie's worth (4 cups) and freeze in individual containers.

Pie crust:

2 ¼ cups flour

8 oz. (one stick) unsalted butter, cut into 8 slices

8 oz. shortening, cut into 8 pieces

½ tsp. salt

Cold water

Mix flour, butter, shortening and salt in food processor a few seconds or by hand, until mixture is the consistency of pea-sized crumbs. Add 8 tbsp. of cold water. Mix a few seconds, just until dough holds together. Divide dough in half. Form each half into a 6-inch disc. Cover well with plastic wrap or place in an airtight container and chill for 20 minutes. Return to room temperature for 5 minutes, and roll out crusts.

Filling:

3 eggs

1 ⅓ cups sugar

3 tbsp. flour

¼ tsp. salt

¼ tsp. cinnamon (or maybe a little more!)

4 cups rhubarb, cut into ½-inch pieces

Mix eggs, sugar, flour, salt and cinnamon. Add rhubarb. Pour filling into pie crust. Cover with top crust. Brush crust with beaten egg yolk or a little cream. Bake in preheated 450° oven for 15 minutes. Reduce heat to 325° and bake for 25 minutes. If not brown enough, turn heat to 425° for 5 minutes or so.

Paul Smith's College student chefs make maple dishes, Paul Smith's College, Paul Smiths. Nancie Battaglia

David Tomberlin is the founder of The Well Dressed Food Company (welldressedfood.com), in Tupper Lake. His business promotes foods grown or prepared in the region, as much as possible.

North Country Rhubarb Sorbet, *David Tomberlin, Tupper Lake*

I want to share this recipe that has become a favorite at our camp. It is a great way to use the rhubarb that becomes abundant in the summer months in the North Country. Even people who don't think they like rhubarb will enjoy this—its great balance of sweet and tangy flavors is very refreshing.

4 cups chopped rhubarb

1 cup water

²/₃ cup sugar

Juice and zest of 2 large oranges

Combine ingredients in a medium saucepan and bring to a boil. Reduce heat to simmer and cook for 20 minutes until rhubarb is soft and tender. Cool and place mixture in a food processor or blender and blend until completely smooth.

Chill for 2 hours or until completely cooled. Process in your ice-cream maker according to manufacturer's directions. Finish freezing in the freezer before serving.

(This is a copyrighted recipe from David's The Well Dressed Food Company that he has graciously shared with us.)

David Tomberlin, of Well Dressed Food, at work in his Tupper Lake kitchen. Nancie Battaglia

Maple Money, *Ellen Rocco, DeKalb*

mong the things I learned from my DeKalb neighbors, Aldena and Milan Conklin, when I first arrived in the North Country, was how to tap maple trees. The Conklins hadn't tapped trees since their children had left home and they were thrilled that newcomers wanted to make syrup. It was a rudimentary system, but it worked. Here's how we did it: About a week before the expected sap run, we jumped in Milan's vintage pickup truck and scoured the roadsides for downed trees, limbs, scrap boards—anything that would burn hot and fast. We laid up a dry cinderblock 3-sided "arch" across the road from my house, just a bit bigger than the flat

Ellen Rocco at her outdoor sugar arch, 1972, DeKalb. Photographer unknown

sugaring pan. With a pole planted at each corner to hold a tarp in the event of rain or snow, we were ready to boil. We had taps, buckets and (some) lids. Buckets were hung up and down the road and off into long-neglected stands of sugar maples. We gathered sap in Milan's milk cans. Let's just say we made dark—very dark—syrup only. Strong and rich with a smoky

Zebr's steaming sugar shack on Route 812, Croghan.
Nancie Battaglia

aroma. After a few years Aldena and Milan bowed out of the process. We were, at least partly, living off the land and decided to try to make some money from the extra syrup. Packaging, we were sure, was the secret. So we canned the syrup in Ball jars, designed homey labels, loaded up our station wagon with dozens of pints and quarts, and headed to New York City. We almost had a success. The buyers at a number of gourmet shops sampled and loved our syrup—and the country packaging. There was one problem: it was spring, of course, because that's when the sap runs. But in New York City we were told people only use syrup in the late fall, as a holiday-related food. Who knew? I grew up in Manhattan. How had I missed this essential fact of city cuisine? We ended up selling our jars from a stand set up in front of a friend's Greenwich Village store. No top-dollar prices but at least we made gas money and didn't have to drive the syrup back home.

Note from Chef George: Before the Europeans brought the honeybee to the New World, the only sweetener available was maple syrup. It takes about 35 gallons of sap to make 1 gallon of syrup. Real maple syrup is expensive, but it's worth it. Once you get used to the real thing it's good-bye to those syrups made with corn syrup.

Maple Syrup Shortcake, *Bryan Thompson, DeKalb*

I'm a sixth-generation northern New Yorker. Here is a recipe from my family of longtime sugar makers.

1 ½ cups maple syrup

2 tsp. baking powder

1 cup flour

¼ tsp. salt

⅓ cup milk

4 tsp. shortening

1 egg

Bring syrup to a boil, then pour into a shallow baking dish. Sift flour, salt and baking powder together in a bowl. Add shortening and blend, but don't overwork. Note: a few pulses in a food processor work well. Finally, beat egg and milk then fold into the flour-shortening mix. Drop from spoon on top of hot syrup and bake at 350° for 25 to 30 minutes. Serve with ice cream.

Serves 4.

Maple Syrup over Biscuits, *Lynn Case Ekfelt, Canton*

One of our favorite desserts in maple syrup season is fresh, homemade biscuits, buttered and broken up in a dish with warm maple syrup poured over them. Sometimes simple is best.

Note from Chef George: The death of biscuits and pie dough is overworking, which builds gluten and makes for a tough final product. My best results have come from cutting cold shortening (or butter) into the flour mixture using a few pulses of a food processor. Dump this mixture into a large bowl and then quickly—and with just a few strokes—mix in the liquid. I always use my hands for this. Don't try and blend it smoothly like in a cake batter. Visible lumps of shortening are fine.

Oxen Bert and Ernie with syrup-maker John Scarlett and his granddaughters, Katarina and Paige, at the end of a long sap freeze-up. Michael O'Dwyer, Rossie. Right: *Bobby's sugar bush, Averyville.* Nancie Battaglia

Maple Haiku Series, *John Scarlett, Rossie*

Under the lid
of a full sap bucket
full moon

Tapping in a spout ...
on the same tree
a woodpecker

Hidden by mist
father and son reminisce
across the evaporator

"Lift me up, Pa"
granddaughter and I
check the buckets

One pint of syrup
equals the five gallons of sap
I just spilled

How rich?
maple syrup
and haiku

Maple Mush, *Maurice Kenny, Saranac Lake*

A n early influence on my culinary ideas and methods was M. F. K. Fisher. In the late 1960s I acquired Fisher's The Art of Eating for $6 in a used bookstore in Brooklyn, where I lived 20 years before returning to the North Country. Ms. Fisher reinforced the idea of respect, not just for prepared food, but also from whence food came: venison from woods, greens from fields, fish from waters, elderberries from forests, sap from trees. She spoke of the lowly potato and how to use foods direct from the meadow, forests, rivers. She also taught how to conserve.

My mother used to make this, which she claimed was an old traditional Iroquois dish.

2 cups water

1 cup yellow cornmeal

A pinch of salt

Butter for sautéing

1 tbsp. maple syrup (more for sweeter teeth)

Bring water to a boil; add cornmeal and salt; cook until thickened, stirring constantly. Remove from heat, spoon into a square container and refrigerate. When ready to serve, strip out the jelled, hardened mush. Slice into ½-inch pieces. Slip into a pan of hot, melted butter and sauté both sides until crisp. (Replacing some of the butter with oil when sautéing raises the smoke point and makes it less likely to burn.) Remove and while still hot pour maple syrup over the cake. Most delicious for breakfast or as a dinner dessert.

Serves 4.

Maple Mousse, *George Arnold, Potsdam*

¼ cup maple syrup

2 egg yolks

1 tsp. unflavored gelatin

1 tbsp. water

½ cup heavy cream

Beat the egg yolks into the maple syrup. Heat slowly over very low heat, stirring constantly until it starts to thicken. Remove from heat. In another bowl, moisten the gelatin with the water, then add it to the maple syrup–egg mixture and stir until dissolved. Cool for about 5 minutes or until it has the consistency of raw egg whites. Whip the heavy cream until it is stiff and fold it into the maple mixture. Put into dishes and cool for at least 3 hours. Wonderful with fresh berries.

Serves 20.

Wax-on-Snow, *Lesley Morse, Copenhagen*

N othing beats maple sugaring in northern New York. Our family visits several sugar bushes in the Croghan area during maple season.

When we return home from the sugar bush with our fresh maple products, we take the maple syrup left over from last year and boil it until it "hairs," which means when you pull the spoon out of the boiling syrup and let it drip, the syrup forms thin hairs. When it "hairs," lightly drizzle the syrup over hardpacked snow in a roasting pan, causing the syrup to hard-

Yancey's maple syrup, Croghan. Nancie Battaglia

en into a taffy, which you then scoop from the snow with a fork, eat and enjoy. To help cut the sweet, my family eats dill pickles along with our wax-on-snow.

Horse-drawn sugar wagon and maple aficionados at Yancey's, Croghan. Nancie Battaglia

Two-Cent Lunch, *Dale Hobson, Potsdam*

I've lost track of how many lunches I have consumed, oblivious at my desk, sandwich in left hand to free my right for the mouse. Lunch is mostly fuel in a working life: nuked leftovers, a pound of takeout swathed in petrochemicals, drive-thru cardiac incidents. It wasn't always so; somewhere I lost the knack for leisure, the rest and playfulness and companionship that once divided the day.

Not that I was ever a café caballero, lingering over lattes and pondering Proust. What I miss is—somebody help me—the elementary school cafeteria. The simplest of fare— brown bag, white bread, gooey peanut butter, purple jelly, milk in a glass bottle, carrot sticks in wax paper, raisins in a cardboard box. And the company of 200 other yammering children. One guy at my table would eat his sandwich down to the shape of a flipped "bird," for the benefit of his recess rivals. Another would squish the whole thing into his mouth at once, roll it into a glutinous ball and display it on extended tongue. I forget why. Carrot sticks

Good food, Raquette Lake. Nancie Battaglia

can double as Dracula fangs. A California raisins box, once empty, makes a dandy kazoo. The uses of a milk straw are too numerous to mention, and the lunch bag itself can be inflated and exploded immediately behind a girl carrying a full tray of spaghetti and meatballs.

It's the greening grass that brings it all to mind, and the memory of milk—two cents for a half-pint bottle, stoppered with a cardboard tab. One day each year it would become transformed from funky white liquid into pure ambrosia, when the local dairyman switched from hay to pasture. You could see the Holstein it came from out the cafeteria window. If you had a good arm, you could hit it with a dried chip from the edge of the schoolyard.

Garden Haiku, *Lucy Martin, Ottawa*

the garden awakes
how can I finish it all?
long days are too short

On a recent North Country Public Radio Readers & Writers on the Air *program, we talked with Michael Pollan about two of his books,* The Omnivore's Dilemma: A Natural History of Four Meals *and* In Defense of Food. *(That program is archived at ncpr.org/readers.) We think his work is a good fit with our book, and asked him if he would provide a few words here. The excerpt below echoes our region's interest in bringing people back to family and community tables and traditions, and back to growing or knowing the growers of our food. Why should a public radio station and Web site care about this? Because we serve a real place, because our ephemeral media is rooted in a living geography. —ER*

Afterword

I'm happy to be included in this book, because it advances the work of rebuilding a local food economy and culture of food.

Without such a thing as fast food there would be no need for slow food, and the stories we tell at such meals would lose much of their interest. Food would be ... well, what it always was, neither slow nor fast, just food: this particular plant or that particular animal, grown here or there, prepared this way or that. For countless generations eating was something that took place in the steadying context of a family and a culture, where the full consciousness of what was involved did not need to be rehearsed at every meal because it was stored away, like the good silver, in a set of rituals and habits, manners and recipes ... Imagine for a moment if we once again knew, strictly as a matter of course, these few unremarkable things: What it is we're eating. Where it came from. How it found its way to our table. And what, in a true accounting, it really cost. We could then talk about some other things at dinner. For we would no longer need any reminding that however we choose to feed ourselves, we eat by the grace of nature, not industry, and what we're eating is never anything more or less than the body of the world.

—Michael Pollan, *from* The Omnivore's Dilemma: A Natural History of Four Meals

Inside the Potsdam Food Co-Op. Nancie Battaglia

Farmers' Markets

FARMERS' MARKET FEDERATION OF NEW YORK *(links to markets by region)*
www.nyfarmersmarket.com/regions.htm

ST. LAWRENCE COUNTY
www.gardenshare.org/farmers_markets.html

JEFFERSON COUNTY
www.comefarmwithus.com/FarmersMarket.htm

ADIRONDACKS

Chateaugay Lakes, Elizabethtown, Keene, Malone, Paul Smiths,
Saranac Lake, Wilmington
www.adirondackfarmersmarket.com

Plattsburgh
www.plattsburghfarmersandcraftersmarket.com
www.plattsburghfarmersmarket.com

Lake Placid
www.lakeplacidmarket.com

SARATOGA SPRINGS AND CLIFTON PARK
www.saratogafarmersmarket.org

VERMONT
www.vermontagriculture.com/buylocal/buy/farmersMarkets.html

ONTARIO

Leeds, Grenville and Frontenac Counties
www.localflavours.org

Community Supported Agriculture

Community Supported Agriculture (CSA) is an arrangement between a farmer and local consumers to share the risks and the bounty of farming. A CSA farm sells shares before each growing season begins and then provides its shareholders with a weekly box of freshly harvested fruits and vegetables throughout the season. The content of a CSA box changes as the season progresses. Some farms provide meat, eggs, honey or maple syrup. More than a dozen farms in the North Country and Adirondacks now offer a CSA option.
www.gardenshare.org/csa_farms.html
www.vermontagriculture.com/buylocal/buy/csa.html

Local Food Resources

Adirondack Harvest focuses on expanding markets for local farm products in Clinton, Essex, Franklin, Hamilton and Warren Counties in northeastern New York. An online search engine helps locate sources for local food in the Adirondacks.
www.adirondackharvest.com

Cornell University Cooperative Extension and the **University of Vermont Extension** provide a wide range of services and resources on agriculture, gardening and nutrition through a network of local offices.
www.cce.cornell.edu
www.uvm.edu/~uvmext

GardenShare works to build a North Country where all of us have enough to eat and enough to share—and where our food choices are healthy for us, for our communities and for the environment. GardenShare maintains an up-to-date listing of Community Supported Agriculture (CSA) farms in the North Country and the Adirondacks and also publishes an annual directory of farm stands, farmers' markets and other outlets for food grown in St. Lawrence County.
www.gardenshare.org

The Northeast Organic Farming Association is an organization of consumers, gardeners and farmers creating a sustainable regional food system that is ecologically sound and economically viable. New York and Vermont each have state chapters.
www.nofany.org
www.nofavt.org

Traditional Arts in Upstate New York (TAUNY) is a nonprofit organization dedicated to documenting, preserving and promoting the folk arts and folklore of New York's North Country. TAUNY published the award-winning cookbook *Good Food, Served Right: Traditional Recipes and Food Customs from New York's North Country.*
www.tauny.org

100-Mile Diet grew out of a one-year experiment by Alisa Smith and James MacKinnon to buy or gather all their food from within 100 miles of their apartment in Vancouver, British Columbia. Their Web site offers resources and suggestions for eating locally across North America.
www.100milediet.org

Community Food Security Coalition unites community gardeners, farmers, anti-hunger advocates, food bankers, nutritionists, public health advocates, environmentalists and churches into a single movement for a socially just and ecologically sustainable food system.
www.foodsecurity.org

Chefs Collaborative is a national network of people in the culinary community who promote sustainable cuisine by celebrating the joys of local and seasonal cooking.
www.chefscollaborative.org

Local Harvest maintains an online directory of small farms, farmers' markets and other local food sources and encourages people to establish direct contact with small farms in their local area.
www.localharvest.org

Slow Food U.S.A. is an educational organization dedicated to the revival of the kitchen and the table as centers of pleasure, culture and community; to the invigoration and proliferation of regional, seasonal culinary traditions; and to living a slower and more harmonious rhythm of life.
www.slowfoodusa.org

—Phil Harnden, *Dekalb, founder,*
GardenShare

Book Resources:

Berry, Wendell. *The Art of the Commonplace: The Agrarian Essays of Wendell Berry*. Shoemaker & Hoard, 2003.

Bourdain, Anthony. *A Cook's Tour*. Bloomsbury, 2001.

Bourdain, Anthony. *Kitchen Confidential: Adventures in the Culinary Underbelly*. Bloomsbury, 2000.

Brillat-Savarin, Jean Anthelme. *The Physiology of Taste*. Heritage Press, 1949.

Brownell, Kelly. *Food Fight: The Inside Story of the Food Industry, America's Obesity Crisis & What We Can Do About It*. McGraw Hill, 2004.

Chaskey, Scott. *This Common Ground: Seasons on an Organic Farm (in Amagansett, NY)*. Viking, 2005.

Culinary Institute of America, The. *Techniques of Healthy Cooking*. Van Nostrand Reynolds, 1993.

Ekfelt, Lynn Case. *Good Food, Served Right: Traditional Recipes and Food Customs from New York's North Country*. Wimmer Books, 2000.

Fisher, M.F.K. *The Art of Eating*. Wiley, 2004.

Gabaccia, Donna. *We Are What We Eat: Ethnic Food and the Making of Americans*. Harvard University Press, 1998.

Gibney, Michael. *Nutrition, Diet & Health*. Cambridge University Press, 1986.

Gifford, K. Dun and Sara Baer-Sinott. *The Oldways Table: Essays and Recipes from the Culinary Think Tank*. Ten Speed Press, 2006.

Halwell, Brian. *Eat Here: Reclaiming Homegrown Pleasures in a Global Supermarket*. Norton/Worldwatch Books, 2004.

Harnden, Philip. *A Gardener's Guide to Frost*. Willow Creek Press, Inc., 2003.

Herbst, Sharon Tyler. *Food Lover's Companion*. Barron's, 2001.

Hockman-Wert, Cathleen and Mary Beth Lind. *Simply in Season*. Herald Press, 2005.

Jones, Evan. *American Food: The Gastronomic Story*. Viking Books, 1981.

Kamp, David. *The United States of Arugula*. Broadway, 2007.

Kingsolver, Barbara. *Animal, Vegetable, Miracle: A Year of Food Life*. HarperCollins, 2007.

Lappe, Frances Moore. *Diet for a Small Planet*. Ballantine, 1991 (updated edition).

Lappe, Frances Moore. *Hope's Edge: The Next Diet for a Small Planet*. Tarcher, 2003.

Lileks, James. *The Gallery of Regrettable Foods*. Crown Publishers, 2001.

Madison, Deborah. *Local Flavors: Cooking and Eating from America's Farmers' Markets*. Broadway, 2002.

Mariani, John F. *The Encyclopedia of American Food and Drink*. Lebhar-Friedman Books, 1999.

McGee, Harold. *On Food and Cooking: The Science and Lore of the Kitchen*. Collier Books, 1984.

McGee, Harold. *The Curious Cook*. Macmillan, 1990.

McKibben, Bill. *Deep Economy: The Wealth of Communities and the Durable Future*. Holt, 2008.

Morash, Marian. *The Victory Garden Cookbook*. Knopf, 1982.

Murray, Sarah. *Movable Feasts: From Ancient Rome to the 21st Century, the Incredible Journeys of the Food We Eat*. St. Martin's Press, 2007.

Pawlick, Thomas F. *The End of Food: How the Food Industry is Destroying Our Food Supply—and What You Can Do About It*. Greystone Books, 2006.

Pollan, Michael. *In Defense of Food*. Penguin Press, 2008.

Pollan, Michael. *The Omnivore's Dilemma: A Natural History of Four Meals*. The Penguin Press, 2006.

Riely, Elizabeth. *The Chef's Companion: A Culinary Dictionary*. John Wiley & Sons, 2003.

Rubin, Martha Adams. *Countryside, Garden and Table: A New England Seasonal Diary*. Golden Co.: Fulcrum Publishing, 1993.

Schlosser, Eric. *Fast Food Nation: The Dark Side of the All-American Meal*. Houghton Mifflin Company, 2001.

Schwabe, Calvin W. *Unmentionable Cuisine*. The University Press of Virginia, 1994.

Schwartz, Joe. *An Apple A Day: The Myths, Misconceptions and Truths About the Foods We Eat*. Harper Collins, 2007.

Singer, Peter. *The Way We Eat: Why Our Food Choices Matter*. Rodale, 2006.

Sizer, Francis and Eleanor Whitney. *Nutrition: Concepts & Controversies*. Wadsworth, 2000.

Sonnenfeld, Albert. *Food: A Culinary History*. Penguin Books, 2000.

Spenser, Colin and Claire Clifton, eds. *The Faber Book of Food*. Faber and Faber, 1993.

Tannahill, Reay. *Food in History*. Three Rivers Press, 1988.

This, Herve and Jody Gladding. *Kitchen Mysteries: Revealing the Science of Cooking*. Columbia University Press, 2007.

Trubek, Amy. *The Taste of Place: A Cultural Journey into Terroir*. University of California Press, 2008.

Visser, Margaret. *The Rituals of Dinner: The Origins, Evolution, Eccentricities, and Meaning of Table Manners*. Penguin Books, 1991.

Winne, Mark. *Closing the Food Gap*. Beacon Press, 2008.

Young, David. *Seasoning: A Poet's Year with Seasonal Recipes*. Ohio State University Press, 1997.

Visit the *Readers & Writers* page on *ncpr.org* for archived conversations with authors of books about food from the 2007–2008 series of programs.

Hikers and canine friends lunching on Hurricane Mt. Nancie Battaglia